teach
yourself

italian phrasebook
vincent edwards and
gianfranca gessa shepheard

For over sixty years, more than
40 million people have learnt over
750 subjects the **teach yourself**
way, with impressive results.

be where you want to be
with **teach yourself**

For UK order enquiries: please contact Bookpoint Ltd, 130 Milton Park, Abingdon, Oxon OX14 4SB. Telephone: +44 (0)1235 827720. Fax: +44 (0)1235 400454. Lines are open 09.00–18.00, Monday to Saturday, with a 24-hour message answering service. Details about our titles and how to order are available at www.teachyourself.co.uk

For USA order enquiries: please contact McGraw-Hill Customer Services, PO Box 545, Blacklick, OH 43004-0545, USA. Telephone: 1-800-722-4726. Fax: 1-614-755-5645.

For Canada order enquiries: please contact McGraw-Hill Ryerson Ltd, 300 Water St, Whitby, Ontario L1N 9B6, Canada. Telephone: 905 430 5000. Fax: 905 430 5020.

Long renowned as the authoritative source for self-guided learning – with more than 30 million copies sold worldwide – the **teach yourself** series includes over 300 titles in the fields of languages, crafts, hobbies, business, computing and education.

British Library Cataloguing in Publication Data: a catalogue record for this title is available from the British Library.

Library of Congress Catalog Card Number: on file.

First published in UK 2004 by Hodder Arnold, 338 Euston Road, London, NW1 3BH.

First published in US 2005 by Contemporary Books, a division of the McGraw-Hill Companies, 1 Prudential Plaza, 130 East Randolph Street, Chicago, IL 60601 USA.

This edition published 2004.

The **teach yourself** name is a registered trade mark of Hodder Headline Ltd.

Authors: Vincent Edwards and Gianfranca Gessa Shepheard

Text and illustrations © Hodder & Stoughton Educational 2004

Printed and bound in Spain.

Impression number 10 9 8 7 6 5 4

Year 2010 2009 2008 2007 2006

CONTENTS

INTRODUCTION	5
PRONUNCIATION GUIDE	7
BASIC EXPRESSIONS	9
ARRIVAL AND DEPARTURE	11
ACCOMMODATION	21

- Hotels
- Camping and caravanning
- Self-catering
- Youth hostels

EATING OUT AND MENU GUIDE	38
ENTERTAINMENT AND SPORT	55
HEALTH	73
TRAVEL	82

- Public transport
- Car
- Breakdown
- Car hire
- Accidents and emergencies
- Boat
- Plane
- Travel in the mountains
- Hitch-hiking
- Pilgrimages
- Disabled travellers

SHOPPING AND SERVICES	107
APPENDIX	124

- Common abbreviations used in Italy
- Time (days, months)
- Italian national holidays
- Distance table
- Metric/imperial conversion table
- Useful addresses
- Telephoning
- Useful telephone numbers

DICTIONARY	138

- English – Italian

INTRODUCTION

The aim of this *Teach Yourself Italian Phrasebook* is to give travellers to Italy, with little or even no knowledge of Italian, an accessible and useful source of Italian words and phrases so that they can draw the maximum advantage from visiting that interesting and beautiful country.

Whether for a tourist or a business person, this book provides a structured grouping of words, phrases, and sentences based on a broad range of general social situations which the traveller might encounter, from arrival at the airport or railway station to getting round Italy successfully. More than that, it gives an insight into things particularly Italian, into what to do in Italy and how to do it, as well as practical hints and useful information.

This phrase book is meant specifically for those travellers who have little or no knowledge of Italian, though the book could also be of interest to more accomplished speakers of the language. The basic structures of Italian introduced here are limited, but sufficient for the traveller to ask meaningful questions and gather useful information. The guide to pronunciation has been developed so that English speakers will find it easy to follow and apply. Unlike English, Italian has a relatively simple phonetic system. The contents list makes it easy to find words for the particular situation you are in, while the general vocabulary at the end is handy for reference.

The important thing is not to worry about accuracy and perfection – this will come with practice – but to have a go, understand and be understood. It is a good idea to study the pronunciation and basic expressions before you set off. In this way you will make the most of your stay in Italy, and while you are there, you will soon find that practice does make perfect and you will build up your knowledge of Italian.

Buon viaggio!

PRONUNCIATION GUIDE

The pronunciation in this phrasebook is indicated by words and syllables easily recognised by English-speaking people. Italian is pronounced as it is written, and every vowel and consonant is fully pronounced and never slurred.

SYMBOL		ITALIAN WORD		ENGLISH WORD
a	*as in*	casa	*compare with*	star
e		mese		get
ee		vivi		eel
o		topo		hot
oo		uva		cool

k	campo	cat
ch	cielo	church
g	gatto	good
j	gentile	judge
LY	aglio	million
NY	ogni	onion
s	santo	sad
sh	scippo	ship
z	scusare	rose
dz	zitella	beds
ts	pizza	vets

A double consonant indicates that the consonant should be intensified: this can change the meaning of the words, eg *capelli* (hair), *cappelli* (hats).

r is pronounced strongly, like the Scottish r.

Italian has a strong stress on each word, the position of which can affect the meaning eg *meta* (aim), *metà* (half). The accent is only written if the stress falls on the final vowel. In the following pages the stressed syllable in each word is indicated with bold type.

h is silent in Italian: it is never pronounced on its own, but is used to give c and g a hard sound.

BASIC EXPRESSIONS

Hello!/Bye!/Hi!/See you!	Ciao! *cheeao!*
Hello/Good morning/afternoon	Buongiorno *boo-onjeeorno*
Good evening	Buona sera *boo-ona sera*
Good night	Buona notte *boo-ona notte*
Goodbye	Arrivederci/Arrivederla *arreevederchee/arreevederla*
How do you do?	Molto lieto/Piacere *molto lee-eto/peeachere*

How are you?	Come stai?/Come sta?/Come va?
	kome staee/kome sta/kome va?
Please	Per piacere/Per favore/
	Per cortesia
	per peeachere/per favore/
	per kortezeea
Excuse me/I'm sorry	Scusi/Scusa
	skoozee/skooza
Thank you	Grazie
	gratsee-e
I would like...	Vorrei...
	vorre-ee...
Where is...?/Where are...?	Dov'è...?/Dove sono...?
	dove...?/dove sono...?
Is there...?/Are there ...?	C'è...?/Ci sono...?
	che...?/chee sono...?
Don't mention it	Prego
(following *grazie*)	*Prego*
I like it/I don't like it	Mi piace/Non mi piace
	mee peeache/non mee peeache

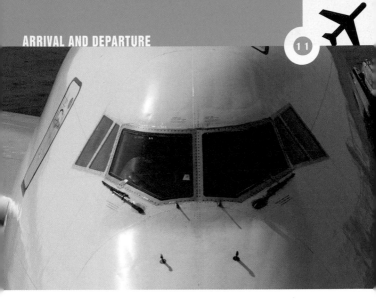

ARRIVAL AND DEPARTURE

Whichever way you enter Italy – by air, land or sea – you will have to go through the usual passport and customs formalities.

At airports and railway stations there will be transport to your destination. If you are using public transport in towns, you may need to buy a ticket before getting on the bus or tram. These tickets are normally available from bars, cafés and tobacconists' shops (*see* **Travel** section, page 82).

Car hire is available in most major towns and points of entry into Italy. See page 95 for details.

BY AIR

aeroplane	l'aeroplano/l'aereo *laeroplano/laereo*
airport	l'aeroporto *laeroporto*
arrivals	gli arrivi *LYee arreevee*
flight	il volo *eel volo*
What time will we get there?	A che ora arriviamo? *a ke ora arreeveeamo?*
Is the plane late/on time?	L'aereo è in ritardo/in orario? *laereo e een reetardo/een orareeo?*
How late is the plane?	Quanto ritardo ha l'aereo? *kooanto reetardo a laereo?*
Is the plane more/less than one hour late?	L'aereo ha più/meno di un'ora di ritardo? *laereo a peeoo/meno dee oonora dee reetardo?*
No smoking	Vietato fumare *vee-etato foomare*
Fasten seat belts!	Allacciare la cintura di sicurezza! *allachcheeare la cheentoora dee seekooretstsa!*
I cannot fasten my seat belt	Non riesco ad allacciarmi la cintura *non ree-esko ad allachcheearmee la cheentoora*
Where do we collect our luggage?	Dove si ritira il bagaglio? *dove see reeteera eel bagaLYeeo?*

BY TRAIN

train	il treno *eel treno*
platform	il binario *eel beenareeo*
railway station	la stazione ferroviaria *la statseeone ferroveeareea*
Where are we?	Dove siamo? *Dove seeamo?*
How many stops before we arrive in...?	Quante fermate ci sono prima di...? *Kooante fermate chee sono preema dee...?*
At what time does the train arrive in...?	A che ora arriva il treno a...? *A ke ora arreeva eel treno a...?*
...Rome	...Roma *roma*
...Milan	...Milano *meelano*
...Naples	...Napoli *napolee*
...Venice	...Venezia *venetseea*
...Florence	...Firenze *feerentse*
...Turin	...Torino *toreeno*
...Genoa	...Genova *jenova*
...Leghorn	...Livorno *leevorno*

BY BOAT

berth	la cuccetta *la koochchetta*
boat	la nave *la nave*
cabin	la cabina *la kabeena*
crossing	la traversata *la traversata*
cruise	la crociera *la krochee-era*
ferry	il traghetto *eel tragetto*
port/harbour	il porto *eel porto*

At what time will the ferry dock?	A che ora arriva il traghetto? *A ke ora arreeva eel tragetto?*
How long is the journey between... and ...?	Quanto dura la traversata fra... e...? *kooanto doora la traversata fra... e...?*
By what time should we leave our cabins?	Entro che ora dobbiamo sgombrare le cabine? *entro ke ora dobbeeamo sgombrare le kabeene?*
When will the car deck be open?	Quando si apre il ponte delle auto? *kooando see apre eel ponte delle aooto?*
Where is cabin number 6 please?	Dov'è la cabina numero sei per piacere? *dove la kabeena noomero se-ee per peeachere?*
I haven't booked a cabin: is there one free?	Non ho prenotato la cabina: ce n'è una libera? *non o prenotato la kabeena: che ne oona leebera?*

PASSPORT CONTROL

customs	la dogana *la dogana*
customs duty	il dazio doganale *eel datseo doganale*
border	il confine *eel konfeene*
customs officer	la guardia di finanza *la gooardeea dee feenantsa*

You may hear:

Apra il cofano per piacere *apra eel kofano per peeachere*	Could you please open the bonnet
È qui per affari o in vacanza? *e kooee per affaree o een vakantsa?*	Are you here on business or on holiday?
È in transito? *e een tranzeeto?*	Are you passing through?
Dov'è diretto? *dove deeretto?*	Where are you going to?
Quanto si trattiene in Italia? *kooanto see trattee-ene een eetaleea?*	How long are you going to stay in Italy?

I'm on my way to the Milan Fair	Sto andando alla Fiera di Milano *sto andando alla fee-era dee meelano*
I'm here on business/holiday	Sono qui per affari/in vacanza *sono kooee per affaree/een vakantsa*
I've nothing to declare	Non ho niente da dichiarare *non o nee-ente da deekeearare*
I'm...	Sono... *sono...*
...British	...britannico/a *breetanneeko/a*

...English	...inglese *eengleze*
...Scottish	...scozzese *skotstseze*
...Irish	...irlandese *eerlandeze*
...Welsh	...gallese *galleze*
...American	...americano/a *amereekano/a*
...Canadian	...canadese *kanadeze*
I am staying for...	Conto di trattenermi... *konto dee trattenermee...*
...one week	...una settimana *oona setteemana*
...a fortnight	...quindici giorni *kooeendeechee jeeornee*
...one month	...un mese *oon meze*
...three months	...tre mesi *tre mezee*
I've only personal things	Ho solo effetti personali *o solo effettee personalee*
Do I have to declare this?	Devo dichiarare questo? *devo deekeearare kooesto?*
How much do I have to pay?	Quando devo pagare? *kooanto devo pagare?*
I have...	Ho... *o...*
...200 cigarettes	...duecento sigarette *dooechento seegarette*

...cigars	...sigari *seegaree*
...perfume	...profumo *profoomo*
...spirits	...liquori *leekoo-oree*
...a bottle of whisky	...una bottiglia di whisky *oona botteeLYeea dee ooeeskee*

LOST PROPERTY

My luggage hasn't arrived yet	I miei bagagli non sono arrivati *ee mee-e-ee bagaLYee non sono arreevatee*
Has the luggage from the London flight arrived?	Sono arrivati i bagagli del volo di Londra? *sono arreevatee ee bagaLYee del volo dee londra?*
I've forgotten my glasses	Ho dimenticato gli occhiali *o deementeekato LYee okkeealee*
Where's the lost property office?	Dov'è l'ufficio oggetti smarriti? *dove looffeecheeo ojjettee smarreetee?*
My name is...	Mi chiamo... *mee keeamo...*
My flight number is...	Il numero del mio volo è... *eel noomero del meeo volo e...*

LUGGAGE COLLECTION

Do we collect our luggage here?	Si ritirano qui i bagagli? *see reeteerano kooee ee bagaLYee?*
This suitcase is mine	Questa valigia è mia *kooesta valeejeea e meea*
Where are the luggage trolleys?	Dove sono i carrelli? *dove sono ee karrellee?*

Where's the way out?	Dov'è l'uscita? *dove loosheeta?*
Where's the information desk?	Dov'è l'ufficio informazioni? *dove looffeecheeo eenformatseeonee?*
Where are the taxis?	Dove sono i taxi? *dove sono ee taxee?*
Where are the buses for the city centre?	Dove sono gli autobus per il centro? *dove sono LYee autoboos per il chentro?*
Where is the bus stop for the air terminal?	Dove si prende l'autobus per il terminal? *dove see prende laootoboos per eel termeenal?*
Is it free?	È gratis? *e gratees?*
How much is it?	Quanto costa? *kooanto kosta?*
Where do I get a ticket for the bus?	Dove si fa il biglietto per l'autobus? *dove see fa eel beeLYee-etto per laootoboos?*
Where's the underground?	Dov'è la metropolitana? *dove la metropoleetana?*
Where can I change some money?	Dove posso cambiare dei soldi? *dove posso kambeeare de-ee soldee?*

DEPARTURE

Departures	le partenze *le partentse*
Where do we check in?	Dove facciamo il check-in? *dove fachcheeamo eel chekeen?*
Am I on stand-by?	Sono in stand-by? *sono een standbaee?*

At what time does flight AB10 leave?	A che ora parte il volo AB10? *a ke ora parte eel volo a bee oono dsero?*
Smoker/Non-smoker	Fumatore/Non fumatore *foomatore/non foomatore*
I would like a seat near a window	Vorrei un posto vicino al finestrino *vorre-ee oon posto veecheeno al feenestreeno*
Here's my ticket/boarding card	Ecco il mio biglietto/ la carta d'imbarco *ekko eel meeo beeLYee-etto/ la karta deembarko*
Can I take this on board?	Posso portare questo sull'aereo? *posso portare kooesto soollaereo?*
I don't have any dangerous articles	Non ho articoli pericolosi *non o arteekolee pereekolozee*
Where's the duty free shop?	Dov'è il duty free shop? *dove eel deeootee free shop?*
Which gate does our flight leave from?	Da che uscita parte il nostro volo? *da ke oosheeta parte eel nostro volo?*
Have they already called flight A213?	Hanno già chiamato il volo A213? *anno jeea keeamato eel volo a dooe oono tre?*
All my clothes are in my suitcase	Tutti i miei vestiti sono nella valigia *toottee ee mee-e-ee vesteetee sono nella valeejeea*
All my work documents	Tutti i miei documenti di lavoro *tootee ee mee-e-ee dokoomentee dee lavoro*

Here's the address of my hotel	Questo è l'indirizzo del mio albergo *kooesto e leendeereetstso del meeo albergo*
Please ring me	Mi telefona per favore? *mee telefona per favore?*
I'm leaving for... in 2 days' time	Fra due giorni parto per... *fra dooe jeeornee parto per...*
I'm staying at the hotel till...	Resto all'albergo fino a... *resto allalbergo feeno a...*
This is my hand luggage	Questo è il mio bagaglio a mano *kooesto e eel meeo bagaLYeeo a mano*
How much do I have to pay for the excess?	Quanto devo pagare per il peso in più? *kooanto devo pagare per eel pezo een peeoo?*
I have a pushchair/wheelchair	Ho un passeggino/una sedia a rotelle *o oon passejjeeno/oona sedeea a rotelle*
Where's the waiting room?	Dov'è la sala d'aspetto/sala d'attesa? *dove la sala daspetto/sala datteza?*
The ferry will leave in half an hour	Il traghetto parte fra mezz'ora *eel tragetto parte fra medsdsora*
Is the sea likely to be smooth or rough?	Il mare sarà calmo o mosso? *eel mare sara kalmo o mosso?*

ACCOMMODATION

Italy has all kinds of accommodation to suit different pockets and inclinations, from campsites and mountain chalets, secluded villas and seaside apartments, to all categories of hotels and boarding houses. Be sure to book in advance during holiday periods and on special occasions such as trade fairs. There are over 40,000 hotels in Italy, classified from one to five stars. The charges of each hotel are agreed with the Provincial Tourist Board and they depend on the locality, the season, the services and the class.

HOTELS AND BOARDING HOUSES

boarding house   la pensione
                                      la penseeone

Be sure to book in advance during holiday periods and on special occasions such as trade fairs.

day hotel [with washing and laundry facilities, often near railway stations]	l'albergo diurno *lalbergo deeoorno*
five star hotel	l'albergo di lusso/ l'albergo di prima categoria *lalbergo dee loosso/ lalbergo dee preema kategoreea*
hotel with/without restaurant	l'albergo con/senza ristorante *lalbergo kon/sentsa reestorante*
youth hostel	l'ostello della gioventù *lostello della jeeoventoo*
entrance	l'ingresso/l'entrata *leengresso/lentrata*
exit	l'uscita *loosheeta*
fire exit	l'uscita di sicurezza *loosheeta dee seekooretstsa*
ground/first/second/third floor	il pianterreno/il primo/ secondo/terzo piano *eel peeanterreno/eel preemo/ sekondo/tertso peeano*
landing	il pianerottolo *eel peeanerottolo*
lift	l'ascensore *lashensore*
reception desk	il banco di reception *eel banko dee reesepshon*
stairs	le scale *le skale*
full board	pensione completa *penseeone kompleta*
half board	mezza pensione *medsda penseeone*

hotel manager	il gestore *eel jestore*
night-porter	il portiere di notte *eel portee-ere dee notte*
receptionist	l'impiegato *leempee-egato*

REGISTERING

You may hear:

Desidera? *dezeedera?*	**Can I help you?**
Ha prenotato? *a prenotato?*	**Have you booked in advance?**
Quanto conta di trattenersi? *kooanto konta dee trattenersee?*	**How long are you staying?**
Camera singola o doppia? *kamera seengola o doppeea?*	**Single or double room?**
Mi favorisce il passaporto? *mee favoreeshe eel passaporto?*	**Could you give me your passport please?**

Have you any vacancies?	Ha delle camere libere? *a delle kamere leebere?*
I have reserved a room for seven days	Ho prenotato una camera per sette giorni *ho prenotato oona kamera per sette jeeornee*
I haven't booked in advance	Non ho già prenotato *non o jeea prenotato*
My travel agent has booked the rooms	L'agenzia di viaggi ha prenotato le camere *lajentseea dee veeajjee a prenotato le kamere*

Here is the confirmation	Ecco la conferma *ekko la konferma*
We would like one double and one single room	Vorremmo una camera matrimoniale e una singola *vorremmo oona kamera matreemoneeale e oona seengola*
single room	una camera singola *oona kamera seengola*
twin-bedded room	una camera a due letti *oona kamera a dooe lettee*
double room	una camera matrimoniale *oona kamera matreemoneeale*
double bed	letto matrimoniale *letto matreemoneeale*
single beds/twin beds	letti singoli/letti gemelli *lettee seengolee/lettee jemellee*
Could you put a third bed in this room?	Potrebbe aggiungere un terzo letto in questa camera? *potrebbe ajjeeoonjere oon tertso letto een kooesta kamera?*
A room with a bath/with a shower	Una camera con bagno/ con doccia *oona kamera kon baNYo/ kon dochcheea*
Is the bathroom on the same floor as the room?	Il bagno è sullo stesso piano della camera? *eel baNYo e soollo stesso peeano della kamera?*
I'd like a room for...	Vorrei una camera per... *vorre-ee oona kamera per...*
...a week	...una settimana *oona setteemana*
...a month	...un mese *oon meze*

...a few days   ...alcuni giorni
alkoonee jeeornee

...one night   ...una notte
oona notte

When you stay in an Italian hotel/boarding house, you have to fill in a registration form (*un modulo*) which includes:

Nome e cognome *nome e koNYome*	**First name and surname**
Data di nascita *data dee nasheeta*	**Date of birth**
Indirizzo *eendeereetstso*	**Address**
Residenza *rezeedentsa*	**Permanent address**
Nazionalità *natseeonaleeta*	**Nationality**
Numero di passaporto *noomero dee passaporto*	**Passport number**
Durata del soggiorno *doorata del sojjeeorno*	**Length of stay**

I have already filled in the form	Ho già compilato il modulo *o jeea compilato eel modoolo*
I don't know how long I'll be staying for	Non so per quanto tempo starò *non so per kooanto tempo staro*
On what floor?	A che piano? *a ke peeano?*
What number?	Che numero? *ke noomero?*

When you stay in an Italian hotel/boarding house, you have to fill in a registration form [*un modulo*]

I'd rather stay in a room on the ground floor or first floor	Preferirei avere una camera al pianterreno o al primo piano *prefereere-ee avere oona kamera al peeanterreno o al preemo peeano*
I cannot climb the stairs for medical reasons	Non posso fare le scale per motivi di salute *non posso fare le skale per moteevee dee saloote*
How much do children pay?	Quanto pagano i bambini? *kooanto pagano ee bambeenee?*
Is there a cot/ a bed for our child?	C'è una culla/ un lettino per il bambino? *che oona koolla/ oon letteeno per eel bambeeno?*
Is breakfast included?	Il prezzo comprende la colazione? *eel pretstso komprende la kolatseeone?*
Is VAT included in the price?	L'IVA è inclusa nel prezzo? *leeva e eenklooza nel pretstso?*
It is too expensive	Costa troppo/È troppo caro *kosta troppo/e troppo karo*
I can't afford it	Non me lo posso permettere *non me lo posso permettere*
Have you got something a bit cheaper?	Avrebbe qualcosa di più economico? *avrebbe kooalkoza dee peeoo ekonomeeko?*
I'd like a room at the front/ at the back of the hotel	Vorrei una camera sul davanti/ sul retro dell'hotel *vorre-ee oona kamera sool davantee/sool retro dellotel*
I'd like to see the room before I make my mind up	Vorrei vedere la stanza prima di decidere *vorre-ee vedere la stantsa preema dee decheedere*

I'll take it	La prendo *la prendo*
I haven't made my mind up yet	Ancora non ho deciso *ankora non o decheezo*
It's too small/too big	È troppo piccola/troppo grande *e troppo peekkola/troppo grande*
Where is the lift?	Dov'è l'ascensore? *dove lashensore?*
Where are the stairs?	Dove sono le scale? *dove sono le skale?*
Where are the fire exits?	Dove sono le uscite d'emergenza in caso d'incendio? *dove sono le oosheete demerjentsa* *een kazo deenchendeeo?*
What is the price...?	Quanto costa...? *kooanto kosta...?*
...per night	...per notte *per notte*
...per week	...per settimana *per setteemana*
...per fortnight	...per due settimane *per dooe setteemane*
How much is full board?	Qual è la tariffa per pensione completa? *kooale la tareeffa per penseeone* *kompleta?*
Is there a discount for...?	C'è lo sconto per...? *che lo skonto per...?*
...children	...bambini *bambeenee*
...students	...studenti *stoodentee*
...pensioners	...pensionati *penseeonatee*

...parties

...comitive
komeeteeve

Are there any facilities for
the disabled?

Ci sono facilitazioni per i
disabili?
*chee sono facheeleetatseeonee per
ee deezabeelee?*

toilets for the disabled

le toilette per disabili
le tooalett per deezabeelee

Is there a ramp for access?

C'è una rampa d'accesso?
che oona rampa dachchesso?

PROBLEMS AND QUESTIONS

My cases are too heavy; could
you help me carry them upstairs?

Le mie valigie sono pesantissime;
mi aiuta a portarle su?
*le mee-e valeejee-e sono
pezanteesseeme; mee aeeoota a
portarle soo?*

I'm sorry, but I have lost my key

Mi spiace, ma ho perso la chiave
*mee speeache, ma o perso la
keeave*

This hotel is too noisy

C'è troppo chiasso in questo
albergo
*che troppo keeasso een kooesto
albergo*

Could I have a quieter room?

Vorrei una camera più tranquilla
*vorre-ee oona kamera peeoo
trankooeella*

Could you wake me up
tomorrow at 6?

Domani mattina può darmi la
sveglia alle sei?
*domanee matteena poo-o darmee
la zveLYea alle se-ee?*

Could we have our passports
back?

Può restituirci i passaporti?
poo-o resteetooeerchee ee passaportee?

Could you call me a taxi for 10.30?	Mi può chiamare un taxi per le dieci e mezza? *mee poo-o keeamare oon taxee per le dee-echee e medsdsa?*
Why is the water off today?	Perché manca l'acqua oggi? *perke manka lakkooa ojjee?*
I do not like the view from my room	Non mi piace la vista dalla mia camera *non mee peeache la veesta dalla meea kamera*
Is there a laundry service in this hotel?	C'è il servizio di lavanderia in questo hotel? *che eel serveetseeo dee lavandereea een kooesto otel?*
Where is the socket for the razor?	Dov'è la presa per il rasoio? *dove la preza per eel razoeeo?*
I need an adaptor for my hair drier/electric razor	Mi occorre un adattatore per il fon/rasoio elettrico *mee okkorre oon adattatore per eel fon/razoeeo elettreeko*
Is there a garage where I can park my car?	C'è una rimessa per parcheggiare la macchina? *che oona reemessa per parkejjeeare la makkeena?*
Here are my car keys	Ecco le chiavi della mia auto *ekko le keeavee della meea aooto*
Where is the nearest bank?	Dove si trova la banca più vicina? *dove see trova la banka peeoo veecheena?*
The air conditioning/ The heating does not work	L'aria condizionata/ Il riscaldamento non funziona *lareea kondeetseeonata/ eel riskaldamento non foontseeona*
The fridge/ The TV set is out of order	Il frigorifero/Il televisore è guasto *eel freegoreefero/eel televeezore e gooasto*

It's too cold in our room and we'd like some extra blankets	Fa troppo freddo in camera e vorremmo altre coperte *fa troppo freddo een kamera e vorremmo altre koperte*
Our room hasn't been cleaned	La nostra camera non è stata pulita *la nostra kamera non e stata pooleeta*
There aren't enough towels in our bathroom	Non ci sono abbastanza asciugamani nel bagno *non chee sono abbastantsa asheeoogamanee nel baNYo*
I'd like to change some traveller's cheques	Vorrei cambiare dei traveller's cheque *vorre-ee kambeeare de-ee travellerz chek*
I'd like to phone this number in England	Vorrei parlare con questo numero in Inghilterra *vorre-ee parlare kon kooesto noomero een eengeelterra*
Can you dial the number for me?	Mi fa il numero? *mee fa eel noomero?*
Can I have an outside line please?	Mi dà una linea per favore? *mee da oona leenea per favore?*
I'd like to check this number in the telephone directory	Vorrei controllare questo numero nell'elenco telefonico *vorre-ee kontrollare kooesto noomero nellelenko telefoneeko*
data transmission line	la linea per trasmissione dati *la leenea per trasmeessee-one datee*
voice box	la casella vocale *la kasella vokale*
check-out 24/7	il check-out 24 ore su 24 *eel chek-aoot venteekooatro ore soo venteekooatro*

interactive satellite TV	la TV satellitare interattiva *la teevoo satelleetare eenteratteeva*
pay TV	la pay-TV *la paee teevoo*
jacuzzi	la vasca per idromassaggio *la vaska per eedromassajjeeo*
rooms for non-smokers	le camere per non fumatori *le kamere per non foomatoree*
TV with videogames	la TV con videogiochi *la teevoo kon veedeojeeokee*
rooms for the disabled	le camere attrezzate per i disabili *le kamere attretstsate per ee deezabeelee*
rooms for the deaf/blind	le camere per gli audiolesi/ non vedenti *le kamere per LYee aoodeeolezee/ non vedentee*
What's the code number for Rome?	Qual è il prefisso per Roma? *kooale eel prefeesso per Roma?*

PAYING THE BILL

I'd like to pay the bill	Vorrei pagare il conto *vorre-ee pagare eel konto*
I'll be leaving at six tomorrow morning: can you have my bill ready?	Partirò alle sei domattina: mi prepara il conto? *parteero alle se-ee domatteena: mee prepara eel konto?*
I must leave at once	Devo partire immediatamente *devo parteere eemmedeeatamente*
We are in a hurry	Abbiamo fretta *abbeeamo fretta*
I believe there's a mistake	Mi sembra che ci sia un errore *mee sembra ke chee seea oon errore*

I'd like to pay in cash/ by credit card/by cheque	Vorrei pagare in contanti/con la carta di credito/con un assegno *vorre-ee pagare een kontante/* *kon la karta dee kredeeto/* *kon oon asseNYo*
Does this bill also include my telephone calls?	Sono incluse anche le mie telefonate in questo conto? *sono eenklooze anke le mee-e* *telefonate een kooesto konto?*
I've already paid for my meals	Ho già pagato per i pasti *o jeea pagato per ee pastee*
I thought meals were included	Pensavo che i pasti fossero inclusi *pensavo ke ee pastee fossero* *eenkloozee*
I've already signed the cheque	Ho già firmato l'assegno *o jeea feermato lasseNYo*
I've signed/filled in the form	Ho firmato/compilato il modulo *o feermato/kompeelato eel modoolo*
signature	la firma *la feerma*
receipt	la ricevuta *la reechevoota*
VAT receipt	la ricevuta fiscale *la reechevoota feeskale*
Can I have a receipt please?	Mi dà la ricevuta per favore? *mee da la reechevoota per favore?*

CAMPING AND CARAVANNING

There are well over 1,600 camping sites in Italy and their prices
vary according to the area and the facilities offered. More
information is available from Centro Internazionale Prenotazioni,
Federcampeggio (Federazione Italiana Campeggiatori), via Vitt.
Emanuele 11, 50041 Calenzano, tel. 055 882391, fax 055
8825918 www.federcampeggio.it

sleeping bag	il sacco a pelo *eel sakko a pelo*
tent	la tenda *la tenda*
Where can we camp for tonight?	Dove possiamo accamparci per stanotte? *dove posseeamo akkamparchee per stanotte?*
bar/hot snack bar	il bar/la tavola calda *eel bar/la tavola kalda*
restaurant	il ristorante *eel reestorante*
shops	i negozi *ee negotsee*
supermarket	il market/il supermercato *eel market/eel soopermerkato*
swimming pool	la piscina *la peesheena*
air mattress	il materassino gonfiabile *eel materasseeno gonfeeabeele*
barbecue	il barbecue *eel barbeekeeoo*
booking	la prenotazione *la prenotatseeone*
camp bed	la brandina *la brandeena*
camper	il campeggiatore *eel kampejjeeatore*
camping site	il campeggio organizzato *eel kampejjeeo organeedsdsato*
caravan	la roulotte/il caravan *la roolot/eel karavan*

caravan driver	il roulottista/il caravanista *eel roolotteesta/eel karavaneesta*
charcoal	la carbonella *la karbonella*
cool bag/cool box	la frigoborsa/la borsa termica *la freegoborsa/la borsa termeeka*
drinking water	l'acqua potabile *lakooa potabeele*
family discount	lo sconto per famiglie *lo skonto per fameeLYee-e*
four-berth caravan	la roulotte a quattro posti/ cuccette *la roolot a kooattro postee/ koochchette*
gas stove	il fornello a gas *eel fornello a gas*
to go camping	fare il campeggio *fare eel kampejjeeo*
inflator	la pompa *la pompa*
picnic/to picnic	il picnic/fare un picnic *eel peekneek/fare oon peekneek*
rucksack	lo zaino *lo dsaeeno*
showers	le docce *le dochche*
What's the charge...?	Qual è la tariffa...? *kooale la tareeffa...?*
...per night	...per notte *per notte*
...per caravan	...per roulotte *per roolot*

...per person	...per persona *per persona*
...per tent	...per tenda *per tenda*
...per car	...per macchina *per makeena*
Where's the nearest camping site?	Dove si trova il campeggio più vicino? *dove see trova eel kampejjeeo peeoo veecheeno?*
We didn't know that camping was not allowed here	Non sapevamo che il campeggio fosse vietato qui *non sapevamo ke eel kampejjeeo fosse vee-etato kooee*
Are there any shopping facilities in the area?	Ci sono dei negozi in zona? *chee sono de-ee negotsee een dsona?*
How far is the lake from the campsite?	Quanto dista il lago dal campeggio? *kooanto deesta eel lago dal kampejjeeo?*
No camping	Vietato il campeggio *vee-etato eel kampejjeeo*
What do we do with the refuse?	Dove buttiamo l'immondizia? *dove bootteeamo leemmondeetseea?*

SELF-CATERING HOLIDAYS

Information on accommodation for self-catering holidays is available from the Tourist Offices (Aziende Autonome di Soggiorno) of the localities chosen, from the Club Alpino Italiano, via E. Petrella 19, 20124 Milano, tel. 02 2057231, fax 02 20572320, website www.cai.it and from Agriturist, corso Vittorio Emanuele 101, 00186 Roma, tel 06/6852342/06 6852337, fax 06 6852424, website www.agriturist.it

apartment	l'appartamento *lappartamento*
bungalow	il bungalow *eel bangalo-oo*
furnished apartment	l'appartamento ammobiliato *lappartamento ammobeeleeato*
We would like to rent the apartment	Vorremmo prendere in affitto l'appartamento *vorremmo prendere een affeetto lappartamento*
What is included in the rent?	Cosa è incluso nell'affitto? *koza e eenkloozo nellaffeetto?*
water	l'acqua *lakkooa*
gas	il gas *eel gas*
electricity	la luce/la corrente *la looche/la korrente*
Do we have to pay separately for...?	Dobbiamo pagare separatamente per...? *dobbeeamo pagare separatamente per...?*
When do the dustmen come?	Quando passano i netturbini? *kooando passano ee nettoorbeenee?*
When does the maid come?	Quando viene la domestica? *kooando vee-ene la domesteeka?*

YOUTH HOSTELS

Information on addresses, membership cards and bookings is available from AIG, Associazione Italiana Alberghi per la Gioventù, via Cavour 44, 00184 Roma, tel 06 4871 52, fax 06 4880492, e-mail aig@uni.net , www.hostels.aig.org and from the Youth Hostel Association, Trevelyan House, Matlock, Derbyshire DE4 3YH, website www.yha.org.uk/

When does the hotel open/close?	Quando apre/chiude l'albergo? *kooando apre/keeoode lalbergo?*
Here is my YHA membership card	Ecco la mia tessera dell'Associazione Alberghi per la Gioventù *ekko la meea tessera dellassocheeatseeone albergi per la jeeoventoo*
Can one eat here?	Si può mangiare qui? *see poo-o manjeeare kooee?*
How many beds are there in each room?	Quanti letti ci sono per camera? *kooantee lettee chee sono per kamera?*
How many nights can I stay?	Quante notti posso restare? *kooante nottee posso restare?*
Can we leave our belongings here during the day?	Possiamo lasciare qui la nostra roba durante il giorno? *posseeamo lasheeare kooee la nostra roba doorante eel jeeorno?*
By what time do we have to clear the room?	Entro che ora dobbiamo sgombrare la stanza? *entro ke ora dobbeeamo sgombrare la stantsa?*

EATING OUT

If you are unsure, let the waiter advise you.

One of the delights of being in Italy is enjoying the rich variety of its food and of its restaurants. These can vary from the peak of high cuisine to modest establishments offering a limited menu. Price, however, is not the sole indicator of culinary excellence and good meals can be obtained in all kinds of settings.

It is difficult to mention specifically *Italian* dishes as the cooking is strongly influenced by regional traditions. If you are unsure, let the waiter advise you.

Main meals in Italy consist of four courses, although you don't have to eat them all! Firstly come antipasti – hors d'oeuvres – often based on either cold sliced meats, salami and various hams or seafood; then there are *primi*, either pasta, rice or soup dishes; *secondi*, the main course, are meat or fish dishes with a *contorno* of vegetables; to finish off there is usually fruit or, somewhat rarely, a dessert.

Smaller restaurants will not necessarily have a printed menu and the waiter will tell you what is available that day.

Enjoy your meal!	Buon appetito! *buoo-on appetteeto!*
restaurant	il ristorante/la trattoria *eel reestorante/la trattoreea*
snack/sandwich bar	la paninoteca/la panineria *la paneenoteka/la paneenereea*
snack bar [hot food]	la tavola calda *la tavola kalda*
pizza restaurant/shop	la pizzeria *la peetstsereea*
take-away pizzeria	la pizzeria da asporto *la peetstsereea da asporto*
take-away food	cibo da asporto *cheebo da asporto*
rotisserie	la rosticceria *la rosteechchereea*
inn/tavern	l'osteria *lostereea*
fast food	fast-food/ristorazione rapida *fast food/reestoratseeone rapeeda*
fast food restaurant	il ristorante fast-food *eel reestorante fast food*
I'm hungry	ho appetito/ho fame *o appeteeto/o fame*
I'm thirsty	ho sete *o sete*

I'm full

sono sazio/sazia
sono satseeo/satseea

GETTING A TABLE

I would like to book a table

Vorrei prenotare un tavolo
vore-ee prenotare oon tavolo

A table for four

Un tavolo per quattro persone
oon tavolo per kooattro persone

A table in the open

Un tavolo all'aperto
oon tavolo allaperto

A table in the shade

Un tavolo all'ombra
oon tavolo allombra

Do you have a table for two?

Avete un tavolo per due?
avete oon tavolo per dooe?

At what time will you have a free table?

A che ora avrete un tavolo libero?
a ke ora avrete oon tavolo leebero?

Can you keep a table for me for this evening?

Mi può riservare un tavolo per stasera?
mee poo-o reezervare oon tavolo per stasera?

Is this place free?

È libero questo posto?
e leebero kooesto posto?

Are these places free?

Questi posti sono liberi?
kooestee postee sono leeberee?

When does this restaurant open?

A che ora apre il ristorante?
a ke ora apre eel reestorante?

Is the restaurant open tomorrow?

Domani il ristorante è aperto?
domanee eel reestorante e aperto?

GETTING A DRINK

Cheers!

Cin Cin!/Salute/Prosit!
cheen cheen!/saloote!/prozeet!

Which soft drinks do you have?	Che bibite/analcolici avete? *ke beebeete/analkoleechee avete?*
wine	vino *veeno*
white wine/red wine	vino bianco/vino rosso *veeno beeanko/veeno rosso*
a fruit juice	un succo di frutta *oon sookko dee frootta*
an orange juice	un succo d'arancia *oon sookko darancheea*
a glass of...	un bicchiere di... *oon beekkee-ere dee...*
...beer	...birra *beerra*
...draught beer	...birra alla spina *beerra alla speena*
...English beer	...birra inglese *beerra eengleze*
...German beer	...birra tedesca *beerra tedeska*
...Italian beer	...birra italiana *beerra eetaleeana*
...cold beer	...birra fresca *beerra freska*
...orangeade	...aranciata *arancheeata*
...lemonade	...gassosa *gassoza*
a grapefruit juice	un succo di pompelmo *oon sookko dee pompelmo*
a pineapple juice	un succo di ananas *oon sookko dee ananas*

an aperitif	un aperitivo
	oon apereeteevo
a vermouth	un vermut
	oon vermoot
a Campari with soda	un Campari con seltz
	oon kamparee kon selts
a non-alcoholic bitter aperitif	un bitter analcolico
	oon beetter analkoleeko
coffee	caffè
	kaffe

There are many kinds of coffee in Italy. If you would like instant, ask for *caffè liofilizzato* (*kaffe leeofeeleedsdsato*).

an espresso coffee	un caffè espresso
	oon kaffe espresso
a very strong black coffee	un caffè ristretto
	oon kaffe reestretto
coffee with milk	caffellatte
	kaffellatte
coffee with a splash of milk	caffè macchiato
	kaffe makkeeato
coffee with a dash of alcohol [eg. grappa, rum, whisky]	caffè corretto
	kaffe korretto
coffee similar to filter coffee	caffè lungo
	kaffe loongo
decaffeinated coffee	caffè decaffeinato
	kaffe dekaffe-eenato
tea with milk/lemon	tè al latte/al limone
	te al latte/al leemone
with/without sugar	con/senza zucchero
	kon/sentsa dsookkero
Can I have some sugar?	Ha dello zucchero?
	a dello dsookkero?

hot chocolate	la cioccolata calda *la cheeokkolata kalda*
a glass of water	un bicchiere d'acqua *oon beekkee-ere dakkooa*
still mineral water	acqua minerale naturale *akkooa meenerale natoorale*
sparkling mineral water	acqua minerale frizzante *akkooa meenerale freetstsante*
ice/ice cubes	il ghiaccio/i cubetti di ghiaccio *eel geeachcheeo/ee koobettee dee geeachcheeo*

MEALS

breakfast	la colazione *la kolatseeone*
lunch	il pranzo *eel prandso*
dinner	la cena *la chena*
snacks	snack/spuntini *snak/spoonteenee*
Is it lunch time?	È l'ora di pranzo? *e lora dee prandso?*
When is dinner?	Quand'è l'ora di cena? *kooande lora dee chena?*

BREAKFAST

Breakfast in Italy is not normally a substantial affair, and many Italians often just grab a coffee and croissant or other pastry in a bar.

A wide range of pastries is usually available in bars and cafés for breakfast: *fritti* (ring doughnuts), *bombe* (doughnuts), *sfoglie* (Palmiers), *cannoli* (filled with cream) and *bignè* (profiteroles).

Another common item in Italian breakfasts are *fette biscottate* (French toast).

coffee and a croissant	caffè/cappuccino e una brioche *kaffe/kappoochcheeno e oona breeosh*
pastry (sweet)	una pasta *oona pasta*
pastry (savoury)	una pizzetta *oona peetstsetta*
Could I have a hot pizzetta?	Mi dà una pizzetta riscaldata, per favore? *mee da oona peetstsetta reeskaldata, per favore?*
What pastries do you have?	Che paste ha? *ke paste a?*
a bread roll	un panino *oon panneeno*
Please bring us some rolls	Ci porti dei panini, per piacere *cee portee de-ee paneenee, per peeachere*
jam	la marmellata *la marmellata*
cherry/peach/apricot jam	la marmellata di ciliege/ pesche/albicocche *la marmellata dee cheelee-eje/ peske/albeekokke*
blackcurrant/raspberry/ strawberry jam	la marmellata di ribes/ lamponi/fragole *la marmellata dee reebes/ lamponee/fragole*
marmalade	la marmellata d'arancia *la marmellata darancheea*
butter	il burro *eel boorro*

SNACKS

You can get a wide variety of snacks in bars, cafés, *tavole calde*, etc.
You normally pay at the cash register and take your receipt
(*scontrino*) to the person behind the counter, telling him or her your
order.

a filled roll	un panino imbottito *oon paneeno eembotteeto*
a roll with cooked ham	un panino con prosciutto cotto *oon paneeno kon prosheeootto kotto*
a roll with raw ham	un panino con prosciutto crudo *oon paneeno con prosheeootto* *kroodo*
a roll with tuna fish	un panino con tonno *oon paneeno kon tonno*
a roll with cheese	un panino con formaggio *oon paneeno kon formajjeeo*
a roll with tomato and mozzarella cheese	un panino con pomodoro e mozzarella *oon paneeno kon pomodoro e* *motstsarella*
a slice of pizza	una fetta di pizza *oona fetta di peetstsa*
a sandwich	un tramezzino *oon trametstseeno*
a toasted sandwich	un to(a)st *oon tost*

ORDERING

What's for lunch?	Cosa c'è a pranzo? *kosa che a prandso?*
Do you have a menu?	C'è un menù? *che oon menoo?*

What are your specialities?	Quali sono le specialità della casa? *kooalee sono le specheealeeta della kaza?*
What are the dishes of the day?	Quali sono i piatti del giorno? *kooalee sono ee peeattee del jeeorno?*
What are the hors d'oeuvres?	Che antipasti ha? *ke anteepastee a?*
What are the first courses?	Cosa c'è per primo? *koza che per preemo?*
What are the second courses?	Cosa c'è per secondo? *koza che per sekondo?*
May I have some fruit?	Vorrei della frutta *vorre-ee della frootta*
May I have some cheese?	Vorrei del formaggio *vorre-ee del formajjeeo*
I don't eat meat	Non mangio mai carne *non manjeeo maee karne*
I'm a vegetarian	Sono vegetariano/vegetariana *sono vejetareeano/vejetareeana*
I'm allergic to...	Sono allergico/allergica a... *sono allerjeeko/allerjeeka a...*
Do you have portions for children?	Fate porzioni speciali per bambini? *fate portseeonee specheealee per bambeenee?*
Is the sauce spicy?	La salsa è piccante? *la salsa e peekkante?*
I don't like spicy sauces	Non mi piacciono le salse piccanti *non mee peeachcheeono le salse peekkantee*
There's too much pepper	C'è troppo pepe *che troppo pepe*

grated cheese	il formaggio grattugiato *eel formajjeeo grattoojjeeato*
a drink after the meal	un digestivo *oon deejesteevo*
bread	il pane *eel pane*
breadsticks	i grissini *ee greesseenee*
cutlery	le posate *le pozate*
knife	il coltello *eel koltello*
fork	la forchetta *la forketta*
spoon	il cucchiaio *eel kookkeeaeeo*
teaspoon	il cucchiaino *eel kookkeeaeeno*
plate	il piatto *eel peeatto*
cup	la tazza/la scodella *la tatstsa/la skodella*
coffee cup	la tazzina da caffè *la tatstseena da kaffe*
saucer	il piattino *eel peeatteeno*
napkin	il tovagliolo *eel tovaLYeeolo*

There are three types of cheese which are normally grated: *parmigiano reggiano* (Parmesan), *grana* (similar to Parmesan) and *pecorino* (made with ewe's milk).

ANTIPASTI   ## HORS D'OEUVRES

You don't have to start with *antipasto*, but their variety and typical Italian composition make an appetising start to a meal.

le cozze/le vongole   mussels/clams
le kotstse/le vongole

i frutti di mare   seafood
ee froottee dee mare

le lumache   snails
le loomake

le olive/le olive farcite   olives/stuffed olives
le oleeve/le oleeve farcheete

il prosciutto affumicato   smoked ham
eel prosheeootto affoomeekato

il prosciutto con melone   ham with melon
eel prosheeootto kon melone

il prosciutto cotto   cooked ham
eel prosheeootto kotto

il prosciutto crudo   raw ham
eel prosheeootto kroodo

il prosciutto di Parma/   Parma ham
San Daniele
eel prosheeootto dee parma/
san danee-ele

i sottaceti/la giardiniera   pickled vegetables
ee sottachetee/la jeeardeenee-era

I PRIMI   ## FIRST COURSE

This is frequently one of the many pasta based dishes, but may be risotto or soup.

il brodo/il consommé   clear soup
eel brodo/eel konsomme

la crema di verdure
la krema dee verdoore

smooth vegetable soup

la frittata
la freettata

omelette with vegetables,
cheese, eggs, breadcrumbs, etc.

le lenticchie/i fagioli/i ceci
*le lenteekkee-e/ee fajeeolee/
ee chechee*

lentils/beans/chick peas

il minestrone
eel meenestrone

vegetable soup

la minestrina in brodo
la meenestreena een brodo

clear soup (with small pasta)

l'omelette
lomlet

omelette

la zuppa di verdure
la dsooppa di verdoore

chunky vegetable soup

I SECONDI

MAIN COURSE

l'agnello/l'abbacchio
laNYello/labbakkeeo

lamb/suckling lamb

le alici/acciughe
le aleechee/achcheeoo-ge

anchovies

al sangue
al sangooe

rare

l'anatra/l'oca
lanatra/loka

duck/goose

l'aragosta/il granchio
laragosta/eel grankeeo

lobster/crab

ben cotto/ben cotta
ben kotto/ben kotta

well done

la bistecca/fettina/
costata/scaloppina

*la beestekka/fetteena/
kostata/skaloppeena*

steak

i calamari/le seppie *ee kalamaree/le seppee-e*	squid
il capretto *eel kapretto*	kid
la carne *la karne*	meat
la carne di cavallo *la karne di kavallo*	horse meat
il coniglio/la lepre *eel koneeLYeeo/la lepre*	rabbit/hare
la cotoletta alla Milanese *la kotoletta alla meelaneze*	cutlet in breadcrumbs
le cotolette/costolette *le kotolette/kostolette*	cutlets
il fagiano *eel fajeeano*	pheasant
il fegato *eel fegato*	liver
i gamberi/i gamberetti *ee gamberee/ee gamberettee*	prawns
il maiale/la porchetta *eel maeeale/la porketta*	pork/suckling pig
il manzo/il vitello *eel mandso/eel veetello*	beef/veal
il merluzzo/il baccalà *eel merlootstso/eel bakkala*	cod/salt cod
il pesce *eel peshe*	fish
il pesce spada/il tonno *eel peshe spada/eel tonno*	swordfish/tuna
il pollo *eel pollo*	chicken

il polpo *eel polpo*	octopus
i rognoni *ee roNYonee*	kidneys
la salsiccia *la salseechcheea*	sausage
le sardine/sardelle *le sardeene/sardelle*	sardines
la sogliola *la soLYeeola*	sole
il tacchino *eel takkeeno*	turkey
la triglia/il muggine *la treeLYeea/eel moojjeene*	red mullet/grey mullet

VINO   WINE

Italy produces a splendid range of wines, many available only in or close to the area where the grapes are cultivated. The initials DOC and DOCG are indicators of quality wines.

abboccato/amabile *abbokkato/amabeele*	sweet
frizzante *freetstsante*	slightly sparkling
rosso/rosato *rosso/rozato*	red/rosé
secco *sekko*	dry
spumante *spoomante*	sparkling
un vino bianco *oon veeno beeanko*	a white wine

un vino bianco secco *oon veeno beeanko sekko*	a dry white wine
il vino della casa *eel veeno della kaza*	house wine
I would like to try...	Vorrei assaggiare... *vorre-ee assajjeeare*
Which wine would you recommend?	Che vino mi consiglia? *ke veeno mee konseelYeea?*
I prefer red wines	Preferisco i vini rossi *prefereesko ee veenee rossee*
I don't like dry wines	Non mi piacciono i vini secchi *non mee peeachcheeono ee veenee sekkee*
Please bring us...	Ci porti per favore... *chee portee per favore...*
a bottle/carafe of	una bottiglia/una caraffa di... *oona botteeLYeea/oona karaffa dee...*
a litre of/half a litre of	un litro di/mezzo litro di... *oon leetro dee/medsdso leetro dee...*
Is this wine strong?	È forte questo vino? *e forte kooesto veeno?*
Could I have another bottle?	Me ne porti un'altra bottiglia *me ne portee oonaltra botteeLYeea*

I CONDIMENTI

l'olio d'oliva
loleeo doleeva

olio e aceto
oleeo e acheto

il parmigiano
eel parmeejeeano

sale e pepe
sale e pepe

CONDIMENTS

olive oil

oil and vinegar

Parmesan

salt and pepper

GELATI

ICE CREAM

Italian ice cream, especially when made on the premises, is delicious and comes in a wide variety of flavours. Pick and mix the flavours (*i gusti*) you like best. *Cassate*, originally from Sicily, are more like ice cream gateaux (*le torte gelato*).

il cornetto/la coppa *eel kornetto/la koppa*	cornet/tub
il frullato/il frappè *eel froollato/eel frappe*	shake
il gelato/la gelateria *eel jelato/la jelatereea*	ice cream/ice cream shop
il ghiacciolo/il sorbetto *eel geeachcheeolo/eel sorbetto*	ice lolly/sorbet
la granita *la graneeta*	crushed ice drink
la panna *la panna*	cream
il semifreddo *eel semeefreddo*	biscuit ice cream
Which flavours do you have?	Che gusti ha? *ke goostee a?*

COMPLAINTS

My plate is dirty	Il mio piatto è sporco *eel meeo peeatto e sporko*
My cutlery is dirty	Le mie posate sono sporche *le mee-e pozate sono sporke*
I don't like this table	Questo tavolo non mi piace *kooesto tavolo non mee peeache*
It's too dark/draughty here	Qui c'è troppo buio/ troppa corrente *kooee che troppo booeeo/ troppa korrente*

I don't want a table near the entrance	Non voglio un tavolo vicino all'entrata *non voLYeeo oon tavolo veecheeno allentrata*
The service is very slow/bad	Il servizio è lentissimo/pessimo *eel serveetseeo e lenteesseemo/ pesseemo*
How long will the next course be?	Quando arriverà la prossima portata? *kooando arreevera la prosseema portata?*
The food is cold	La roba da mangiare è fredda *la roba da manjeeare e fredda*
It isn't cooked/it's still raw	Non è cotto/è ancora crudo *non e kotto/e ankora kroodo*
We didn't order this	Non abbiamo ordinato questo *non abbeeamo ordeenato kooesto*
There's an error in the bill	C'è uno sbaglio sul conto *che oono zbaLYeeo sool konto*
I refuse to pay for this	Mi rifiuto di pagare questo *mee reefeeooto dee pagare kooesto*

ENTERTAINMENT AND SPORT

Italy offers a broad range of entertainment in a typically Italian way. Whether you are interested in sport, or the arts, or folklore, there is so much to see and do.

In holiday resorts night life tends to be lively. If you are after more traditional forms of entertainment, then you can go to the theatre or opera. Even smallish towns have their own theatre, which is normally a source of civic pride. In summer performances may be in the open air. This also applies to films.

If you get the chance, spare some time for popular festivals – both religious and secular. They are still an important part of life in Italy today.

Most churches and cathedrals are open to the public for viewing, except during services. You should obtain permission to take photos and should not enter the church in inappropriate attire.

Most churches and cathedrals are open to the public for viewing, except during services. You should obtain permission to take photos and should not enter the church in inappropriate attire.

CINEMA

actor/actress	l'attore/l'attrice *lattore/lattreeche*
black and white film	il film in bianco e nero *eel feelm een beeanko e nero*
continuous performance	il programma continuo *eel programma konteenoo-o*
cinema [building]	il cinema *eel cheenema*
multiplex cinema	il multiplex *eel moolteepleks*
18-screen multiplex	il multiplex con 18 schermi *eel moolteepleks kon deecheeotto skermee*
director	il regista cinematografico *eel rejeesta cheenematografeeko*
film	il film *eel feelm*
thriller	il thriller *eel treller*
usherette	la maschera *la maskera*
western	il western *eel ooestern*
Coming soon!	Imminente! *eemmeenente!*

No admission to people younger than 18	Vietato ai minori di 18 anni *vee-etato aee meenoree dee deecheeotto annee*
For children	Per bambini *per bambeenee*
I'd like three tickets	Vorrei tre biglietti *vorre-ee tre beeLYee-ettee*
At what time does the film start?	A che ora comincia il film? *a ke ora komeencheea eel feelm?*
At what time is the last performance?	A che ora comincia l'ultimo spettacolo? *a ke ora komeencheea loolteemo spettakolo?*
How long is the film?	Quanto dura il film? *kooanto doora eel feelm?*
I'd like to sit at the back/front	Vorrei un posto nelle file di dietro/davanti *vorre-ee oon posto nelle feele dee dee-etro/davantee*
Is the cinema air-conditioned?	C'è l'aria condizionata nel cinema? *che lareea kondeetseeonata nel cheenema?*
Do you have reductions for children and OAPs?	Ci sono sconti per i bambini e i pensionati? *chee sono skontee per ee bambeene e ee penseeonatee?*

THEATRE

audience	il pubblico *eel poobbleeko*
box office	il botteghino *eel bottegeeno*

circle	la galleria
	la gallereea
comedian	il comico
	eel komeeko
curtain	il sipario
	eel seepareeo
farce	la farsa
	la farsa
musical	la commedia musicale
	la kommedeea moozeekale
open-air theatre	il teatro all'aperto
	eel teatro allaperto
play	la commedia
	la kommedeea
show	lo spettacolo
	lo spettakolo
sold out	tutto esaurito
	tootto ezaooreeto
stage	il palcoscenico
	eel palkosheneeko
stalls	la platea
	la platea
tragedy	la tragedia
	la trajedeea
I'd like to book three seats for the 21st	Vorrei prenotare tre posti per il ventuno
	vorre-ee prenotare tre postee per eel ventoono
I'd like two tickets for the stalls please	Due biglietti di platea per favore
	dooe beeLYee-ettee dee platea per favore

Do we have to buy the tickets in advance?

Dobbiamo fare i biglietti in anticipo?
dobbeeamo fare ee beeLYee-ettee een anteecheepo?

FOLKLORE

celebration

il festeggiamento
eel festejjeeamento

folk dance

l'antico ballo popolare
lanteeko ballo popolare

folk song

il canto popolare
eel kanto popolare

patron saint of a town

il santo patrono della città
eel santo patrono della cheetta

patron saint festival

la festa patronale
la festa patronale

procession

la processione
la prochesseeone

country festival

la festa campestre
la festa kampestre

traditional regional costumes

i costumi regionali tradizionali
ee kostoomee rejeeonalee tradeetseeonalee

village festival

la sagra del paese
la sagra del paeze

village square

la piazza del paese
la peeatstsa del paeze

When is the next patron saint celebration of this village?

Quando sarà la prossima festa patronale di questo paese?
kooando sara la prosseema festa patronale dee kooesto paeze?

I'd like to listen to some local folk music

Vorrei ascoltare della musica tradizionale
vorre-ee askoltare della moozeeka tradeetseeonale

Are there any local handicraft shops?

Ci sono dei negozi di artigianato locale?
chee sono de-ee negotsee dee arteejeeanato locale?

MONUMENTS AND BUILDINGS

amphitheatre

l'anfiteatro
lanfeeteatro

archaeological remains/ excavations

i resti archeologici/
gli scavi archeologici
ee restee arkeolojeechee/
LYee skavee arkeolojeechee

castle

il castello
eel kastello

cathedral

la cattedrale/il duomo
la kattedrale/eel doo-omo

cemetery

il cimitero/il camposanto
eel cheemeetero/eel kamposanto

church

la chiesa
la kee-eza

city walls

le mura della città
le moora della cheetta

fortress

la fortezza
la fortetstsa

old town centre

il centro storico
eel chentro storeeko

monument

il monumento
eel monoomento

ruins

i ruderi
ee rooderee

sculpture

la scultura
la skooltoora

statue	la statua *la statooa*
When was this church built?	A quando risale la costruzione di questa chiesa? *a kooando reesale la kostrootseeone dee kooesta kee-eza?*
What does that monument commemorate?	Che cosa commemora quel monumento? *ke koza kommemora kooel monoomento?*
Could you tell me the way to the Roman ruins and temple?	Sa dirmi come arrivare ai ruderi e al tempio romani? *sa deermee kome arreevare aee rooderee e al tempeeo romanee?*
I'd like to buy a map of the old town	Vorrei comprare una cartina del centro storico *vorre-ee komprare oona karteena del chentro storeeko*
Are cars allowed into the town centre?	Le macchine hanno l'accesso al centro? *le makkeene anno lachchesso al chentro?*

MUSEUMS AND GALLERIES

exhibition	la mostra/l'esposizione *la mostra/lespozeetseeone*
museum of archaeology	il museo archeologico *eel moozeo arkeolojeeko*
museum of modern art	il museo d'arte moderna *eel moozeo darte moderna*
painter	il pittore/la pittrice *eel peettore/la peettreeche*
painting	la pittura/il dipinto *la peettoora/eel deepeento*

picture/picture gallery	il quadro/la pinacoteca *eel kooadro/la peenakoteka*
portrait	il ritratto *eel reetratto*
still life	la natura morta *la natoora morta*
How much is the entrance fee to the museum?	Quanto costa il biglietto d'ingresso al museo? *kooanto kosta eel beeLYee-etto deengresso al moozeo?*
Is it free for children?	L'ingresso è gratis per i bambini? *leengresso e gratees per ee bambeenee?*
Is this museum open every day?	Questo museo è aperto tutti i giorni? *kooesto muzeo e aperto toottee ee jeeornee?*
Is the picture gallery open at lunch time?	La pinacoteca è aperta all'ora di pranzo? *la peenakoteka e aperta allora dee prandso?*
I'd like to see some archaeological exhibits	Vorrei vedere dei reperti archeologici *vorre-ee vedere de-ee repertee arkeolojeechee*

MUSIC

ballet	il balletto *eel balletto*
band	la banda/l'orchestrina *la banda/l'orkestreena*
chamber music	la musica da camera *la moozeeka da kamera*

classical music	la musica classica *la moozeeka klasseeka*
composer	il compositore *eel kompozeetore*
conductor	il direttore d'orchestra *eel deerettore dorkestra*
concert/concert hall	il concerto/la sala dei concerti *eel koncherto/la sala de-ee konchertee*
musical instruments	gli strumenti musicali *LYee stroomentee moozeekalee*
musical season	la stagione musicale *la stajeeone moozeekale*
open-air concert	il concerto all'aperto *eel koncherto allaperto*
opera	l'opera/la lirica *lopera/la leereeka*
orchestra	l'orchestra *lorkestra*
pop group	il complesso pop/il complesso rock *eel komplesso pop/eel komplesso rok*
pop music	la musica pop *la moozeeka pop*
garage music, techno music	la musica garage, la musica techno *la moozeeka garaj, la moozeeka tekno*
record/cassette/videotape/ CD/DVD	il disco/la cassetta/il videotape/ il CD/il DVD *eel deesko/la kassetta/eel videote-eep/ eel chee dee/eel dee vee dee*
record/cassette/ CD player/DVD player	il giradischi/il mangianastri/ il lettore di CD/il lettore di DVD *eel jeeradeeskee/eel manjeeanastree/ eel lettore dee chee dee/eel lettore dee dee vee dee*

walkman/discman	il walkman/il discman *eel walkman/eel deeskman*
singer/to sing	il cantante/cantare *eel kantante/kantare*
soloist/choir	il solista/il coro *eel soleesta/eel koro*
soprano/alto/tenor/baritone	il soprano/il contralto/ il tenore/il baritono *eel soprano/eel kontralto/ eel tenore/eel bareetono*
symphony	la sinfonia *la seenfoneea*
What's on tonight at the Conservatoire?	Cosa c'è in programma al Conservatorio stasera? *koza che een programma al konservatoreeo stasera?*
Who is the conductor?	Chi dirige l'orchestra? *kee deereeje lorkestra?*
Where can I find some information on summer concerts?	Dove posso trovare delle informazioni sui concerti di quest'estate? *dove posso trovare delle eenformatseeonee sooee konchertee dee kooestestate?*
Will there be many open-air concerts?	Ci saranno molti concerti all'aperto? *chee saranno moltee konchertee allaperto?*
Where can I find a record shop?	Dove trovo un negozio di dischi? *dove trovo oon negotseeo dee deeskee?*

NIGHTLIFE

to dance	ballare *ballare*
dinner dance	la serata danzante *la serata dantsante*
discotheque	la discoteca *la deeskoteka*
nightclub	il nightclub/il locale notturno *eel naeetklab/eel locale nottoorno*
How much is the entrance fee for two?	Quanto costa per due? *kooanto kosta per dooe?*
Are drinks included/excluded?	Le bibite sono incluse/escluse? *le beebeete sono eenkloose/eskloose?*
Who's singing tonight?	Che cantante c'è stanotte? *ke kantante che stanotte?*
At what time will the club close tonight?	A che ora si chiude stanotte il nightclub? *a ke ora see keeoode stanotte eel naeetklab?*

RADIO AND TELEVISION

In Italy the state television RAI – Radiotelevisione Italiana – has three channels. There are many private radio and television stations as well as regional networks.

cartoons	i cartoni animati *ee kartonee aneematee*
current affairs	l'attualità *lattooaleeta*
documentary	il documentario *eel dokoomentareeo*
film made for television	il telefilm *eel telefeelm*

news	le notizie *le noteetsee-e*
programme	il programma *eel programma*
private radio/TV station	la radio privata/la TV privata *la radeeo preevata/la teevoo preevata*
satellite TV/cable TV/Pay-TV	la TV satellitare/la TV via cavo/ la Pay-TV *la tee-voo satelleetare/la tee-voo veea kavo/la pe-ee tee-vee*
radio news	il giornale radio/il notiziario *eel jeeornale radeeo/ eel noteetseeareeo*
show	lo spettacolo *lo spettakolo*
soap opera	la soap opera/la telenovela *la sop opera/la telenovela*
state radio/TV	la radio di stato/la TV di stato *la radeeo dee stato/la teevoo dee stato*
subtitles	le didascalie/i sottotitoli *le deedaskalee-e/ee sottoteetolee*
weather forecast	le previsioni del tempo *le preveezeeonee del tempo*
I'd like to watch the television news	vorrei vedere il telegiornale *vorre-ee vedere eel telejeeornale*
Which is the best private TV station?	Qual è la migliore TV privata? *kooale la meeLYeeore teevoo preevata?*
Are there any English programmes?	Ci sono dei programmi in inglese? *chee sono de-ee programmee een eengleze?*

Has that programme got English subtitles?	Quel programma ha le didascalie in inglese? *kooel programma a le deedaskalee-e een eengleze?*

READING

In Italy there are several daily papers, both independent and party ones, some sport and many regional daily papers. The number of weekly, fortnightly and monthly publications is endless and covers every interest, from current affairs, politics and gossip, to business, marketing and computers.

book/bookshop	il libro/la libreria *eel leebro/la leebrereea*
comic	il fumetto *eel foometto*
detective novel	il romanzo giallo/il romanzo poliziesco *eel romandso jeeallo/eel romandso poleetsee-esko*
dictionary	il dizionario/il vocabolario *eel deetseeonareeo/eel vokabolareeo*
fiction	la narrativa *la narrateeva*
library	la biblioteca *la beebleeoteka*
magazine	la rivista/il rotocalco *la reeveesta/eel rotokalko*
newsagent	l'edicola/il chiosco *ledeekola/eel keeosko*
newspaper	il giornale/il quotidiano *eel jeeornale/eel koo-oteedeeano*
novel	il romanzo *eel romandso*

romance	il romanzo rosa *eel romandso roza*
poetry/poem	la poesia *la poezeea*
writer	lo scrittore/la scrittrice *lo skreettore/la skreettreeche*
I'd like a copy of today's sports paper	Un quotidiano sportivo per favore *oon koo-oteedeeano sporteevo per favore*
Is this the latest edition of this book?	Questa è l'ultima edizione di questo libro? *kooesta e loolteema edeetseeone dee kooesto leebro?*
Where are the English books?	Dove sono i libri in inglese? *dove sono ee leebree een eengleze?*
Do you have any English newspapers?	Vende dei giornali inglesi? *vende de-ee jeeornalee eengleze?*
Where can I purchase an English newspaper?	Dove posso comprare un giornale inglese? *dove posso komprare oon jeeornale eengleze?*

RELAXATION, REST AND HOBBIES

In some parts of Italy it is a widespread custom for people to go out late in the afternoon and walk with their friends along the main street for *la passeggiata*.

holiday/vacation	le vacanze/la villeggiatura *le vakantse/la veellejjeeatoora*

In some parts of Italy it is a widespread custom for people to go out late in the afternoon and walk with their friends along the main street for *la passeggiata*.

holiday resort	il luogo di villeggiatura *eel loo-ogo dee veellejjeeatoora*
Where do young people meet for the local *passeggiata*?	Dove s'incontrano i giovani per la passeggiata? *dove seenkontrano ee jeeovanee per la passejjeeata?*
summer/winter holidays	la villeggiatura estiva/invernale *la veellejjeeatoora esteeva/eenvernale*
aerobics/to do aerobics	l'aerobica/fare l'aerobica *laerobeeka/fare laerobeeka*
fishing/to go fishing	la pesca/andare a pescare *la peska/andare a peskare*
I'd like to go to the beach	Vorrei andare alla spiaggia/al mare *vorre-ee andare alla speeajjeea/al mare*
I have a rest/relax/sleep	Mi riposo/Mi rilasso/Dormo *mee reepozo/mee reelasso/dormo*
jogging	il footing/il jogging *eel footeen/eel joggeen*
mountain climbing	l'alpinismo *lalpeeneezmo*
ornithology	l'ornitologia *lorneetolojeea*
photography	la fotografia *la fotografeea*
I play cards/draughts/chess/football	Gioco a carte/a dama/a scacchi/a calcio *jeeoko a karte/a dama/a skakkee/a calcheeo*
I play the guitar/piano/violin	Suono la chitarra/il piano/il violino *soo-ono la keetarra/eel peeano/eel veeoleeno*

See also section on Group Travel, page 102.

I play video games/
computer games

Gioco a videogame/
Gioco col computer
*jeeoko a veedeoge-eem/
jeeoko kol kompee-ooter*

I like surfing the Net/chatting
on the Net

Mi piace navigare in
Internet/chattare su
Internet
*mee peeache naveegare een
eenternet/chattare soo
eenternet*

stamp collecting

la filatelia
la feelateleea

Is there a gym/fitness
centre nearby?

C'è una palestra/un
centro fitness qui vicino?
*che oona palestra/oon
chentro feetnes koo-ee
veecheeno?*

hobby

l'hobby/il passatempo
lobbee/eel passatempo

SIGHTSEEING

day trip

la gita
la jeeta

itinerary

l'itinerario
leeteenerareeo

tour

il giro turistico
eel jeero tooreesteeko

tourist

il/la turista
eel/la tooreesta

tourist information centre

il centro informazioni
turismo
*el chentro eenformatseeonee
tooreezmo*

When is the tour starting?	Quando comincia il giro turistico? *kooando komeencheea eel jeero tooreesteeko?*
Can we have a packed lunch there?	Potremo mangiare al sacco lì? *potremo manjeeare al sakko lee?*

SPORT

athletics	l'atletica leggera *latleteeka lejjera*
basketball	la pallacanestro/il basket *la pallakanestro/eel basket*
boxing	il pugilato/la boxe *eel poojeelato/la box*
championship	il campionato *eel kampeeonato*
cup/trophy/medal	la coppa/il trofeo/la medaglia *la koppa/eel trofeo/la medaLYee-a*
match	la partita/l'incontro *la parteeta/leenkontro*
motor racing track	l'autodromo *laootodromo*
player	il giocatore/la giocatrice *eel jeeokatore/la jeeokatreeche*
racecourse [for horse racing]	l'ippodromo *leeppodromo*
referee/linesman	l'arbitro/il guardialinee *larbeetro/eel gooardeealeenee*
sports arena	il palazzetto dello sport *eel palatstsetto dello sport*
stadium	lo stadio *lo stadeeo*

team	la squadra *la skooadra*
How much is the admission ticket?	Quanto costa il biglietto d'ingresso? *kooanto kosta eel beeLYee-etto deengresso?*
Where can I buy two tickets for tonight's match?	Dove posso acquistare due biglietti per la partita di stasera? *dove posso akooeestare dooe beeLYee-ettee per la parteeta dee stasera?*
Which teams are playing tomorrow at the stadium?	Che squadre giocano domani allo stadio? *ke skooadre jeeokano domanee allo stadeeo?*
Who won last year's championship/football league?	Chi ha vinto il campionato/lo scudetto dell'anno scorso? *kee a veento eel kampeeonato/lo skoodetto dellanno skorso?*
I support my local team	Faccio il tifo per la mia squadra locale *fachcheeo eel teefo per la meea skooadra lokale*

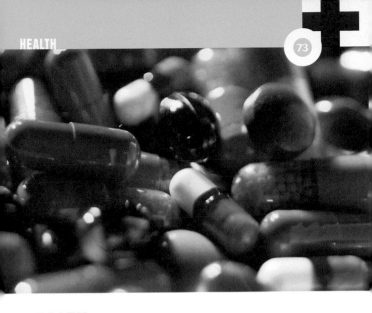

HEALTH

Italy offers many opportunities for staying, or getting, fit and healthy.
The dietary benefits of Italian food and cooking are widely
recognised. The climate and landscape encourage a range of physical
activities from swimming to mountaineering, or even just sightseeing.
Whatever you choose to do, do not overdo the sun.
As both Italy and the United Kingdom are members of the EU,
visitors can benefit from the health services available to Italians.
Form E111 and further information can be obtained from offices of
the Department of Health and the Post Office.

My ... hurts	Mi fa male... *mee fa male...*
I can't move my ...	Non posso muovere... *non posso moo-overe...*

THE HUMAN BODY

back	la schiena *la skee-ena*
chest	il petto *eel petto*
ear/ears	l'orecchio/le orecchie *lorekkeeo/le orekkee-e*
eye	l'occhio *lokkeeo*
face	la faccia/il viso *la fachcheea/eel veezo*
finger/toe	il dito della mano/il dito del piede *eel deeto della mano/eel deeto del pee-ede*
hand/wrist	la mano/il polso *la mano/eel polso*
foot/ankle	il piede/la caviglia *eel pee-ede/la kaveeLYeea*
head	la testa/il capo *la testa/eel kapo*
heart	il cuore *eel koo-ore*
leg	la gamba *la gamba*
lungs	i polmoni *ee polmonee*
knee/knees	il ginocchio/le ginocchia *eel jeenokkeeo/le jeenokkee-a*
mouth	la bocca *la bokka*
neck	il collo *eel kollo*
shoulder	la spalla *la spalla*

| stomach | lo stomaco |
| | *lo stomako* |

AT THE DOCTOR'S

| doctor's surgery | l'ambulatorio |
| | *lambulatoreeo* |

| Excuse me, is there a surgery nearby? | Scusi, c'è un ambulatorio qui vicino? |
| | *skoozee che oon amboolatoreeo kooee veecheeno?* |

| Could you call a doctor, please? | Può chiamare il medico per favore? |
| | *poo-o keeamare eel medeeko per favore?* |

| I feel ill | Mi sento male/Non mi sento bene |
| | *mee sento male/non mee sento bene* |

| I have been feeling ill for several days | Sto male da parecchi giorni |
| | *sto male da parekkee jeeornee* |

| I've had a temperature for two days | Ho la febbre da due giorni |
| | *o la febbre da dooe jeeornee* |

| Is my prescription ready? | La mia ricetta è pronta? |
| | *la meea reechetta e pronta?* |

| My throat is burning | Mi brucia la gola |
| | *mee broocheea la gola* |

| I've had diarrhoea and nausea all night | Ho avuto la diarrea e la nausea tutta la notte |
| | *o avooto la deearrea e la naoozea tootta la notte* |

| I have been sick several times | Ho vomitato varie volte |
| | *o vomeetato varee-e volte* |

| I have a migraine | Ho l'emicrania |
| | *o lemeekraneea* |

| I am allergic to penicillin | Sono allergico alla penicillina |
| | *sono allerjeeko alla peneecheelleena* |

I have diabetes/haemophilia	Ho il diabete/l'emofilia *o eel deeabete/lemofeeleea*
I'm HIV positive	Sono sieropositivo *sono see-eropozeeteevo*
I have asthma	Sono asmatico *sono azmateeko*
I've sprained my wrist/ankle	Mi sono slogato/slogata il polso/la caviglia *mee sono zlogato/zlogata eel polso/ la kaveeLYeea*
I have a...	Ho mal... *o mal...*
...headache	...di testa *dee testa*
...earache	...d'orecchio *dorekkeeo*
...stomach ache	...di stomaco *dee stomako*

You may hear:

Si spogli per favore *see spoLYee per favore*	Could you undress, please?
Apra la bocca *apra la bokka*	Open your mouth, please
Tossisca *tosseeska*	Cough, please
Respiri profondamente *respeeree profondamente*	Take a deep breath
Le fa male qui? *le fa male kooee?*	Does it hurt here?
Dove le fa male? *dove le fa male?*	Where does it hurt?
È bene che lei faccia delle analisi *e bene ke le-ee fachheea delle analeezee*	You should have some tests

PAYING

How much do I owe you?	Quanto le devo? *kooanto le devo?*
Is your fee paid by my insurance?	La sua parcella è pagata dalla mia assicurazione? *la sooa parchella e pagata dalla meea asseekooratseeone?*
Could you give me a receipt for my insurance?	Mi dà una ricevuta per l'assicurazione? *mee da oona reechevoota per lasseekooratseeone?*

AILMENTS

AIDS	l'AIDS *la ee-dee-esse*
cancer	il cancro *eel kankro*
cold/cough	il raffreddore/la tosse *eel raffreddore/la tosse*
I have a very heavy cold	sono costipato/constipata *sono kosteepato/kosteepata*
constipation/I am constipated	la stitichezza/sono stitico/stitica *la steeteeketstsa/sono steeteeko/ steeteeka*
diabetes	il diabete *eel deeabete*
diarrhoea/vomiting	la diarrea/il vomito *la deearrea/eel vomeeto*
dizzy spells/vertigo	i capogiri/le vertigini *ee kapojeeree/le verteejeenee*
I have food poisoning	ho l'intossicazione *o leentosseekatseeone*
heart attack	l'infarto/il collasso cardiaco *leenfarto/eel kollasso kardeeako*

high/low blood pressure	la pressione alta/bassa *la presseeone alta/bassa*
bite	la puntura/il pizzico *la poontoora/eel peetstseeko*
I've been stung by a wasp	Mi ha punto una vespa *mee a poonto oona vespa*
burn	l'ustione/la scottatura/ la bruciatura *loosteeone/la skottatoora/* *la broocheeatoora*
sunstroke	l'insolazione *leensolatseeone*
cut	il taglio/la ferita *eel taLYeeo/la fereeta*

FOR WOMEN

period	la mestruazione *la mestrooatseeone*
I have period pains	Soffro di mestruazioni dolorose *soffro dee mestrooatseeonee doloroze*
the Pill	la pillola anticoncezionale *la peellola anteekonchetseeonale*
the morning after pill	la pillola del giorno dopo *la peellola del jeeorno dopo*
emergency contraception	la contraccezione d'emergenza *la kontrachchetseeone demerjentsa*
I'm pregnant	Sono incinta/Aspetto un bambino *sono eenchenta/aspetto oon bambeeno*
I have lost the pills I normally take	Ho perso le pastiglie che prendo di solito *o perso le pasteeLYee-e ke prendo* *dee soleeto*

I have morning sickness	Ho la nausea *o la naoozea*
My baby is due in six weeks' time	Il bambino dovrebbe nascere fra sei settimane *eel bambeeno dovrebbe nashere fra se-ee setteemane*

AT THE CHEMIST'S

chemist's	la farmacia *la farmacheea*
prescription	la ricetta medica *la reechetta medeeka*
aspirin	l'aspirina *laspeereena*
antibiotic	l'antibiotico *lanteebeeoteeko*
condoms	i profilattici/i preservativi/ i condom *ee profeelatteechee/ee prezervateevee/ ee kondom*
contraceptives	gli antifecondativi/ gli anticoncezionali *LYee anteefekondateevee/ LYee anteekonchetseeonalee*
cough mixture	lo sciroppo contro la tosse *lo sheeroppo kontro la tosse*
painkiller	il calmante/l'analgesico *eel kalmante/lanaljezeeko*
How much is the prescription charge?	Quanto costa il ticket? *kooanto kosta eel teeket?*
Could I have some throat lozenges?	Vorrei delle pastiglie per la gola *vorre-ee delle pasteeLYee-e per la gola*

Can you recommend some tablets for an upset stomach?

Può darmi delle compresse per il mal di stomaco?
Poo-o darmee delle kompresse per eel mal dee stomako?

You may hear:

Da prendersi tre volte al giorno con i pasti
da prendersee tre volte al jeeorno kon ee pastee

To be taken three times a day with meals

Da prendersi dopo i pasti
da prendersee dopo ee pastee

To be taken after meals

Da non prendersi con bevande alcolich
da non prendersee kon bevande alkoleeke

Not to be taken with alcohol

AT THE DENTIST'S

dentist

il/la dentista
eel/la denteesta

tooth/toothache/tooth decay

il dente/il mal di denti/ la carie
eel dente/eel mal dee dentee/ la karee-e

I have toothache

Ho mal di denti
o mal dee dentee

My denture is broken

La mia dentiera è rotta
la meea dentee-era e rotta

I'm going to have a tooth filled

Devo farmi otturare un dente
devo farmee ottoorare oon dente

Do you have to pull this tooth out?

Deve proprio estrarre questo dente?
deve propreeo estrarre kooesto dente?

AT THE OPTICIAN'S

optician

l'oculista/l'ottico
lokooleesta/lotteeko

contact lenses

le lenti a contatto
le lentee a kontatto

frame/spectacles

la montatura/gli occhiali
la montatoora/LYee okkeealee

I am longsighted/shortsighted

Sono presbite/miope
sono prezbeete/meeope

My spectacles are broken

I miei occhiali sono rotti
ee mee-e-ee okkealee sono rottee

In Italy the *Oculista* carries out the eye test and gives the patient a prescription. The *Ottico* sells frames and lenses and fits the glasses according to the prescription.

TRAVEL

There's so much to see in Italy that you will need to get around if you want to make the most of your stay. Italy has one of the best motorway networks in Europe as well as an extensive system of public transport.

Buses and trains are relatively inexpensive. In cities remember to buy your ticket (available from tobacconists and newsagents) before getting on the bus or tram. In most big towns the same tickets are used on all public transport and a ticket normally allows unlimited travel in a city for up to two hours. You can buy single (*biglietto per una corsa*) and multiple tickets (*biglietto per sei/dodici corse*) which are then punched by the machines on buses, trams, etc.

PUBLIC TRANSPORT

bus	l'autobus *laootoboos*
coach	il pullman *eel poollman*
tram	il tram *eel tram*
trolleybus	il filobus *eel feeloboos*
train	il treno *eel treno*
commuter train	il treno dei pendolari *eel treno de-ee pendolaree*
local train	il treno locale *eel treno locale*
long distance train (stopping at all the major stations)	il diretto *eel deeretto*
express train (with fewer stops than the *diretto*)	l'espresso/il direttissimo *lespresso/eel deeretteesseemo*
first/second class	prima/seconda classe *preema/sekonda klasse*
carriage	la carrozza/il vagone *la karrotstsa/eel vagone*
railway station	la stazione ferroviaria *la statseeone ferroveeareea*

In cities remember to buy your ticket (available from tobacconists and newsagents) before getting on the bus or tram. In most big towns the same tickets are used on all public transport and a ticket normally allows unlimited travel in a city for up to two hours. You can buy single (*biglietto per una corsa*) and multiple tickets (*biglietto per sei/dodici corse*) which are then punched by the machines on buses, trams, etc.

restaurant car	la carrozza ristorante
	la karrotstsa reestorante
From which platform does it leave?	Da che binario parte?
	da ke beenareeo parte?

BUSES AND COACHES

bus/tram/trolleybus stop	la fermata dell'autobus/ del tram/del filobus
	la fermata dellaootoboos/ del tram/del feeloboos
bus/tram terminus	il capolinea
	eel kapoleenea
Where do the buses/coaches/ trams for... leave from?	Da dove partono gli autobus/ i pullman/i tram per...?
	da dove partono LYee aootoboos/ ee poollman/ee tram per...?
Do the coaches have toilets/ air conditioning?	Sulle corriere ci sono le toilette/ c'è l'aria condizionata?
	soolle korree-ere chee sono le tooalet/che lareea kondeetseeonata?
At what time do coaches leave for...?	A che ora partono i pullman per ...?
	a ke ora partono ee poollman per...?
Can I reserve a seat/seats?	Posso prenotare un posto/dei posti?
	posso prenotare oon posto/de-ee postee?
How long is the journey to...?	Quanto si impiega ad arrivare a...?
	kooanto see eempee-ega ad arreevare a...?
Where does the coach stop?	Dove si ferma il pullman?
	dove see ferma eel poollman?
At what time does the coach return from...?	A che ora il pullman ritorna da...?
	a ke ora eel poollman reetorna da...?
Where's the bus stop?	Dov'è la fermata dell'autobus?
	dove la fermata dellaootoboos?

BUYING A TICKET

Where's the ticket office?	Dov'è la biglietteria? *dove la beeLYee-ettereea?*
Where's the ticket machine?	Dov'è la biglietteria automatica? *dove la beeLYee-ettereea aootomateeka?*
Where can you buy tickets for the bus?	Dove si comprano i biglietti per l'autobus? *dove see komprano ee beeLYee-ettee per laootoboos?*
Do you sell tickets for the bus?	Vende biglietti per l'autobus? *vende beeLYee-ettee per laootoboos?*
I'd like a ticket for six journeys	Un biglietto per sei corse per favore *oon beeLYee-etto per se-ee korse per favore*
How much is a ticket?	Quanto costa un biglietto? *kooanto kosta oon beeLYee-etto?*
A ticket to... please	Un biglietto per..., per piacere *oon beeLYee-etto per..., per peeachere*
A single ticket for...	Un biglietto di sola andata per... *oon beeLYee-etto dee sola andata per*
A return ticket	Un biglietto di andata e ritorno *oon beeLYee-etto dee andata e reetorno*
sleeper	il vagone letto *eel vagone letto*
I am travelling tomorrow/the day after tomorrow/the 8th August	Parto domani/dopodomani/l'otto agosto *parto domanee/dopodomanee/lotto agosto*

Can I break my journey at...?	È possibile interrompere il viaggio a...? *e posseebeele eenterrompere eel veeajjeeo a...?*
Can I go direct to...?	Si può andare direttamente a...? *see poo-o andare deerettamente a...?*
How long do I have to wait for a connection to...?	Quanto dovrò aspettare la coincidenza per...? *kooanto dovro aspettare la koeencheedentsa per...?*
Could I have a train timetable?	Mi dà un orario dei treni per favore? *mee da oon orareeo de-ee trenee per favore?*
How long is this ticket valid for?	Per quanto tempo è valido questo biglietto? *per kooanto tempo e valeedo kooesto beeLYee-etto?*
Can I walk there?	Ci si arriva a piedi? *chee see arreeva a pee-edee?*
Do I have to get a bus?	Devo prendere l'autobus? *devo prendere laootoboos?*
Which number?/Which route?	Che numero prendo?/Che linea? *kee noomero prendo?/ke leenea?*
Where's the nearest bus stop?	Dov'è la fermata d'autobus più vicina? *dove la fermata daootoboos peeoo veecheena?*

BY CAR

If you do not have one of the new EU licences, your UK driving licence must be accompanied by a translation (obtainable free of charge from the AA, RAC, ENIT, Italian Tourist Office, or ACI, Italian Automobile Association).

You are advised to obtain a Green Card to make sure that you have comprehensive insurance. It is also advisable to check before travelling with the above organisations regarding the latest regulations. You should note that no motor traffic is permitted in some city centres on Sundays.

You may see:

Dare la precedenza	**Give way**
Divieto d'accesso	**No entry**
Zona pedonale	**Pedestrian precinct**
Senso unico	**One way street**
Divieto di sorpasso	**No overtaking**
Limite di velocità	**Speed limit**
Evitare i rumori molesti	**Do not use car horn**

How do I get to...?	Come si arriva a...? *kome see arreeva a...?*
Can you give me some directions to...?	Mi sa dire come arrivare a...? *mee sa deere kome arreevare a...?*
right	destra *destra*
left	sinistra *seeneestra*
straight on	sempre diritto *sempre deereetto*
Do I turn right?	Giro a destra? *jeero a destra?*

 If you do not have one of the new EU licences, your UK driving licence must be accompanied by a translation (obtainable free of charge from the AA, RAC, ENIT, Italian Tourist Office, or ACI, Italian Automobile Association).

North/East/South/West	Nord/Est/Sud/Ovest *nord/est/sood/ovest*
by-pass	la circonvallazione *la cheerkonvallatseeone*
city policeman/policewoman	il vigile/la vigilessa *eel veejeele/la veejeelessa*
crossroad/junction	l'incrocio *leenkrocheeo*
direction indicator	la freccia direzionale *la frechcheea deeretseeonale*
fork (in road)	il bivio *eel beeveeo*
intersection	lo svincolo *lo zveenkolo*
lane (of road)	la corsia *la korseea*
pavement	il marciapiedi *eel marcheeapee-edee*
pedestrian	il pedone *eel pedone*
policeman	il poliziotto *eel poleetseeotto*
road/street	la strada *la strada*
road open to heavy traffic	la strada camionabile *la strada kameeonabeele*
road sign	il cartello/il segnale stradale *eel kartello/eel seNYale stradale*
traffic jam	l'ingorgo *leengorgo*
traffic lights (red/amber/green)	il semaforo (rosso/giallo/verde) *eel semaforo (rosso/jeeallo/verde)*
zebra crossing	il passaggio pedonale *eel passajjeeo pedonale*

| There is a lot of traffic | C'è tanto traffico |
| | *che tanto traffeeko* |

PROBLEMS AND QUESTIONS

If you are stopped by the police following an infringement you will be asked to show your documents: *Favorisca i documenti*.

I documenti are: driving licence, insurance and car ownership papers.

I didn't see the STOP sign	Non avevo visto lo STOP
	non avevo veesto lo stop
I hadn't realised my tyres were bald	Non sapevo che le gomme fossero liscie
	non sapevo ke le gomme fossero leeshee-e
I didn't notice the one way sign	Non ho visto il senso unico
	non ho veesto eel senso ooneeko
What is the speed limit here?	Qual è il limite di velocità qui?
	kooale eel leemeete dee velocheeta kooee?
I didn't know parking was not allowed	Non sapevo che non si potesse parcheggiare
	non sapevo ke non see potesse parkejjeeare
fine	la multa/la contravvenzione
	la moolta/la kontravventseeone
Do I have to pay a fine?	Devo pagare la multa?
	devo pagare la moolta?
Parking	Parcheggio
	parkejjeeo
No parking	Sosta vietata
	sosta vee-etata
car park	il parcheggio
	eel parkejjeeo

parking disc	il disco orario *eel deesko orareeo*
disc car park	il parcheggio a disco orario *eel parkejjeeo a deesko orareeo*
parking meter	il parchimetro *eel parkeemetro*
supervised car park	il parcheggio custodito *eel parkejjeeo koostodeeto*
Is there a car park nearby?	C'è un parcheggio qui vicino? *che oon parkejjeeo kooee veecheeno?*

MOTORWAYS AND MAJOR ROADS

On Italian motorways, tolls are charged in most cases. On entering
the motorway the driver obtains a ticket which is surrendered at the
exit gate where the toll is calculated and paid. The charge is based
on the kilometres covered and on the capacity of the vehicle.
Payment can be in cash, by credit card or by Viacard, similar to a
phone card, available from stationers and shops displaying the
Viacard sign on the door. On some sections of motorway a flat toll is
charged and this is payable on entry.

'A' road	la statale (SS on maps) *la statale*
'B' road	la provinciale *la proveencheeale*
carriageway	la carreggiata *la karrejjeeata*
dual carriageway	la superstrada *la sooperstrada*
motorway	l'autostrada *laootostrada*
motorway emergency lane	la corsia d'emergenza dell'autostrada *la korseea demerjentsa dellaootostrada*

motorway exit	il raccordo d'uscita *eel rakkordo doosheeta*
service area	l'area di servizio *larea dee serveetseeo*
toll gate	il casello *eel kazello*
toll motorway	autostrada a pedaggio/ a pagamento *aootostrada a pedajjeeo/ a pagamento*
toll-free motorway	autostrada libera *aootostrada leebera*
How much is it from... to...?	Quanto costa da... a...? *kooanto kosta da... a...?*
Where can I get on the motorway?	Dov'è il raccordo d'entrata? *dove eel rakkordo dentrata?*
Where's the next exit?	Dov'è la prossima uscita? *dove la prosseema oosheeta?*

You may see:

Veicoli lenti	**Slow moving vehicles**
Solo sorpasso	**Overtaking only lane**
Marcia normale	**Normal speed lane**
Sosta d'emergenza	**Emergency lane**
Divieto di sorpasso	**No overtaking**

 On Italian motorways, tolls are charged in most cases. On entering the motorway the driver obtains a ticket which is surrendered at the exit gate where the toll is calculated and paid. The charge is based on the kilometres covered and on the capacity of the vehicle. Payment can be in cash or by Viacard, similar to a phone card, available from stationers and shops displaying the Viacard sign on the door. On some sections of motorway a flat toll is charged and this is payable on entry.

Nowadays only unleaded petrol (benzina verde) and diesel are available.

Where can I call the assistance service?	Da dove si chiama il soccorso stradale? *da dove see keeama eel sokkorso stradale?*
petrol station	il distributore/il benzinaio/ la stazione di servizio *eel destreebootore/eel bendseenaeeo/la statseeone dee serveetseeo*
petrol	la benzina/il carburante *la bendseena/eel karboorante*
diesel	il gasolio/il diesel *eel gazoleeo/eel deezel*
unleaded petrol	la benzina senza piombo/ verde *la bendseena sentsa peeombo/ verde*
Fill her up!	Mi faccia il pieno! *mee fachcheea eel pee-eno!*
Could I have... Euros' worth of unleaded, please?	Mi dà... Euro di benzina verde, per favore... *mee da... eooro dee bendseena verde, per favore*
Could you check the oil/the tyres?	Dà una controllata all'olio/ alle gomme? *da oona kontrollata alloleeo/ alle gomme?*
Could you give the windscreen a wash?	Mi pulisce il parabrezza? *mee pooleeshe eel parabretstsa?*
Which petrol stations are open?	Quali sono i distributori di turno? *kooalee sono ee deestreebootoree dee toorno?*

BREAKDOWN

To obtain help in case of breakdown, dial 116.

A red reflector triangle (*il triangolo*) must be displayed in case of breakdown to warn other drivers of one's presence.

My car has broken down	La mia auto è guasta/ è in panne *la meea aooto e gooasta/ e een panne*
accelerator	l'acceleratore *lachcheleratore*
brake/hand brake	il freno/il freno a mano *eel freno/eel freno a mano*
car window	il finestrino *eel feenestreeno*
clutch	la frizione *la freetseeone*
gearbox	il cambio *eel kambeeo*
fog lamps	i fari antinebbia *ee faree anteenebbeea*
full-beam headlights	gli abbaglianti *LYee abbaLYeeantee*
dipped headlights	gli anabbaglianti *LYee anabbaLYeeantee*
horn	il clackson *eel klakson*
jack	il cric *eel kreek*
radiator	il radiatore *eel radeeatore*

To obtain help in case of breakdown, dial 116.
A red reflector triangle (*il triangolo*) must be displayed in case of breakdown to warn other drivers of one's presence.

rear-view mirror	lo specchietto retrovisore *lo spekkee-etto retroveezore*
steering wheel	il volante *eel volante*
suspension	la sospensione *la sospenseeone*
spare tyre	la ruota di scorta *la roo-ota dee skorta*
windscreen	il parabrezza *eel parabretstsa*
windscreen wiper	il tergicristallo *eel terjeekreestallo*
air/oil filter	il filtro dell'aria/dell'olio *eel feeltro dellareea/delloleeo*
carburettor	il carburatore *eel karbooratore*
fuel injection	l'iniezione di carburante *leenee-etseeone dee karboorante*
fan belt	la cinghia del ventilatore *la cheengeea del venteelatore*
exhaust pipe	la marmitta/il tubo di scappamento *la marmeetta/eel toobo dee scappamento*
catalytic converter	il catalizzatore *eel kataleedsdsatore*
spark plugs	le candele *le kandele*
starter motor	lo starter *lo starter*
I've got a puncture	Ho una gomma a terra *ho oona gomma a terra*
The headlights aren't working	I fari non funzionano *ee faree non foontseeonano*

The battery is flat	La batteria è scarica *la battereea e skareeka*
Is there a garage nearby?	C'è un'officina qui vicino? *che oonoffeecheena kooee veecheeno?*
Could you have a look at my car?	Può vedere cosa c'è che non va nella mia macchina? *poo-o vedere koza che ke non va nella meea makkeena?*
Have you managed to repair the fault?	È riuscito a riparare il guasto? *e reeoosheeto a reeparare eel gooasto?*
Is it serious?	È una cosa grave? *e oona koza grave?*
Will you order the spare parts?	Deve ordinare i pezzi di ricambio? *deve ordeenare ee petstsee dee reekambeeo?*
When will my car be ready?	Quando sarà pronta la mia macchina? *kooando sara pronta la meea makkeena?*

CAR HIRE

car hire	l'autonoleggio *laootonolejjeeo*
I would like to hire a car	Vorrei noleggiare un'auto *vorre-ee nolejjeeare oonaooto*
I'd like a big/small car	Vorrei un'auto di grande/piccola cilindrata *vorre-ee oonaooto dee grande/peekkola cheeleendrata*
I'd like a comfortable car	Vorrei un'auto comoda *vorre-ee oonaooto komoda*
I'd like a sports/fast car	Vorrei un'auto sportiva/veloce *vorre-ee oonaooto sporteeva/veloche*

I'd like an automatic/ economical car	Vorrei una macchina automatica/ economica *vorre-ee oona makkeena aootomateeka/ekonomeeka*
driving licence	la patente di guida *la patente dee gooeeda*
valid/not valid driving licence	la patente valida/scaduta *la patente valeeda/skadoota*
insurance	l'assicurazione *lasseekooratseeone*
unlimited mileage	chilometraggio illimitato *keelometrajjeeo eelleemeetato*
Is insurance/VAT included?	L'assicurazione/l'IVA è inclusa? *lasseekooratseeone/ leeva e eenklooza?*
Are there any additional costs?	Ci sono delle spese extra? *chee sono delle speze extra?*
Is the car new/in good condition?	La macchina è nuova/in buone condizioni? *la makkeena e noo-ova/een boo-one kondeetseeonee?*
What's the total cost?	Quanto viene a costare in tutto? *kooanto vee-ene a kostare een tootto?*
When/Where can I collect the car?	Quando/Dove posso ritirare la macchina? *kooando/dove posso reeteerare la makkeena?*
Where can I return the car/ the keys?	Dove devo riconsegnare la macchina/le chiavi? *dove devo reekonseNYare la makkeena/le keeavee?*
Do I need to fill in a form?	Devo riempire un modulo? *devo ree-empeere oon modoolo?*

Do I pay in advance?	Pago in anticipo? *pago een anteecheepo?*
Can you give me a route map?	Avrebbe una carta stradale? *avrebbe oona karta stradale?*
Can my husband/wife/son/ daughter also drive?	Può guidare anche mio marito/ mia moglie/mio figlio/mia figlia? *poo-o gooeedare anke meeo mareeto/* *meea moLYee-e/ meeo feeLYeeo/meea* *feeLYeea?*
What will you do if I have an accident/if I break down?	Cosa farete in caso di incidente/ di guasto? *koza farete een kazo dee eencheedente/* *dee gooasto?*
The tank is almost full	Il serbatoio è quasi pieno *eel serbatoeeo e kooazee pee-eno*
Car radio	l'autoradio *laootoradeeo*

ACCIDENTS AND EMERGENCIES

112 and 113 are the Italian equivalents of the British 999 to call the carabinieri and the police respectively.

115 is the number for the fire service (*i vigili del fuoco/i pompieri*) or an ambulance (*l'ambulanza*).

118 is the number for all medical emergencies.

car crash	lo scontro *lo skontro*
dead/injured/unharmed	morto/ferito/illeso *morto/fereeto/eellezo*
head-on collision	lo scontro frontale *lo skontro frontale*
I've run somebody over	Ho investito una persona *o eenvesteeto oona persona*

That car went into the back of mine	Quella macchina mi ha tamponato *kooella makkeena mee ha tamponato*
He didn't give way	Non mi ha dato la precedenza *non mee a dato la prechedentsa*
The accident occurred as I was pulling out of this road	Si è verificato l'incidente mentre uscivo da questa strada *see e vereefeekato leencheedente mentre oosheevo da kooesta strada*
I was backing out of this road	Facevo la retromarcia da questa via *fachevo la retromarcheea da kooesta veea*
traffic	il traffico *eel traffeeko*
to overtake	sorpassare/superare *sorpassare/sooperare*
assistance service	il soccorso stradale *eel sokkorso stradale*

BY WATER

canal	il canale navigabile *eel kanale naveegabeele*
ship	la nave/il piroscafo *la nave/eel peeroskafo*
berth	la cuccetta/la cabina *la koochchetta/la kabeena*
ferry boat	il traghetto *eel tragetto*

112 and 113 are the Italian equivalents of the British 999 to call the carabinieri and the police respectively.
115 is the number for the fire service (*i vigili del fuoco/i pompieri*) or an ambulance (*l'ambulanza*).
118 is the number for all medical emergencies.

gondola	la gondola *la gondola*
hovercraft	l'hovercraft *loverkraft*
hydrofoil	l'aliscafo *laleeskafo*
quay	il molo *eel molo*
How long is the crossing?	Quanto dura la traversata? *kooanto doora la traversata?*
Where do we get off?	Dove si sbarca? *dove see sbarka?*
calm/rough sea	mare calmo/mare mosso *mare kalmo/mare mosso*
Where can I buy some sea sickness tablets?	Dove posso comprare delle pastiglie contro il mal di mare? *dove posso komprare delle pasteeLYee-e kontro eel mal dee mare?*
Where does the steamer stop?	Dove si ferma il vaporetto? *dove see ferma eel vaporetto?*
Is it possible to hire a motor boat?	Si può noleggiare un motoscafo? *see poo-o noljjeeare oon motoskafo?*

RESCUE

Help!	Aiuto! *aeeooto!*
Coast Guard	la Guardia Costiera *la gooardeea kostee-era*
life boat	la scialuppa di salvataggio *la sheealooppa dee salvatajjeeo*
life jacket	il bagnino *eel baNYeeno*

SOS	SOS (Soccorso Occorre Subito)
	esse o esse
Beware of the rocks!	Attenti agli scogli!
	attentee aLYee skoLYee!

BY AIR

aeroplane	l'aereo
	laereo
glider	l'aliante
	laleeante
hang glider	il deltaplano
	eel deltaplano
helicopter	l'elicottero
	leleekottero
hot air balloon	la mongolfiera/
	il pallone aerostatico
	la mongolfee-era/
	eel pallone aerostateeko
light aircraft	l'aereo da turismo
	laereo da tooreezmo
supersonic jet	il jet supersonico
	eel jet soopersoneeko

IN THE MOUNTAINS

cable car	la funivia/la teleferica
	la fooneeveea/la telefereeka
chair lift	la seggiovia
	la sejjeeoveea
funicular	la funicolare
	la fooneekolare
ski lift	la sciovia
	la sheeoveea

How far does the road go?	Fin dove arriva la strada? *feen dove arreeva la strada?*
Is the road open/closed?	La strada è aperta/chiusa al traffico? *la strada e aperta/keeooza al traffeeko?*
Is the pass open?	Il valico è aperto? *eel valeeko e aperto?*
Is there much snow/ice on the road?	C'è molta neve/molto ghiaccio sulla strada? *che molta neve/molto geeachcheeo soolla strada?*
Do I need snow chains?	Mi servono le catene? *mee servono le katene?*
Mont Blanc tunnel	il tunnel del Monte Bianco *eel toonnel del monte beeanko*
St Bernard tunnel	il tunnel del San Bernardo *eel toonnel del san bernardo*
avalanche	la valanga *la valanga*
landslide	la frana *la frana*
How can one get to the peak?	Come si arriva alla vetta/alla cima? *kome see arreeva alla vetta/alla cheema?*
glacier	il ghiacciaio *eel geeachcheeaeeo*
volcano	il vulcano *eel voolkano*
Can one visit the crater?	Si può arrivare al cratere? *see poo-o arreevare al kratere?*
Is the volcano still active?	Il vulcano è sempre attivo? *eel voolkano e sempre atteevo?*

HITCH-HIKING

hitch-hiking	l'autostop *laootostop*
I'd like to go to Rome. How far are you going?	Vorrei andare a Roma. Fin dove arriva lei? *vorre-ee andare a roma.* *feen dove arreeva le-ee?*
Could you give me a lift as far as...?	Mi dà un passaggio fino a...? *mee da oon passajjeeo feeno a...?*

GROUP TRAVEL

courier	il/la rappresentante/ il corriere *eel/la rapprezentante/* *eel korree-ere*
guide	la guida *la gooeeda*
interpreter	l'interprete *leenterprete*
I'm one of the... group	Faccio parte della comitiva... *fachcheeo parte della komeeteeva...*
Where/When do we meet up again?	Dove/Quando dobbiamo rincontrarci? *dove/kooando dobbeeamo reenkontrarchee?*
Do we meet again here?	Dobbiamo ritrovarci qui? *dobbeeamo reetrovarchee kooee?*

Have you seen our courier?	Avete visto il nostro corriere? *avete veesto eel nostro korree-ere?*
Would it be possible...?	Sarebbe possibile...? *sarebbe posseebeele...?*
...to stay longer in...	...prolungare la visita a... *proloongare la veezeeta a...*
...to return earlier from...	...rientrare prima da... *ree-entrare preema da...*
bicycle	la bicicletta *la beecheekletta*
motorbike/motorcycle	la motocicletta *la motocheekletta*
tandem	il tandem *eel tandem*

PILGRIMAGES

pilgrim	il pellegrino *eel pellegreeno*
We are going on a pilgrimage	Andiamo in pellegrinaggio *andeeamo een pellegreenajjeeo*
basilica	la basilica *la bazeeleeka*
blessing	la benedizione *la benedeetseeone*
convent	il convento *eel konvento*
monastery	il monastero *eel monastero*
Pope	il Papa *eel papa*
prayer	la preghiera *la pregee-era*

procession	la processione
	la prochesseeone
saints	i santi
	ee santee
shrine	il santuario
	eel santooareeo
the Vatican	il Vaticano
	eel vateekano
candle	la candela
	la kandela
We want to go to an audience with the Pope	Vorremo andare ad un'udienza del Papa
	vorremmo andare ad oonoodee-entsa del papa

FOR DISABLED TRAVELLERS

Information is available from RADAR – Royal Association for Disability and Rehabilitation – 12 City Forum, 250 City Road, London EC1V 8AF. Tel. +44 (0)207 250 3222, www.radar.org.uk

disabled people	i disabili/le persone disabili
	ee deezabeelee/le persone deezabeelee
crutches	le stampelle/le grucce
	le stampelle/le groochche
walking stick/zimmer frame	il bastone/il girello
	eel bastone/eel jeerello
wheelchair	la carrozzina a rotelle/ la sedia a rotelle
	la karrotstseena a rotelle/ la sedeea a rotelle
tourism for disabled people	turismo accessibile
	tooreesmo achchesseebeele
services for disabled people	servizi per i disabili
	serveetsee per ee deezabeelee

tourist services for disabled people	servizi turistici accessibili per i disabili *serveetsee tooreesteechee achchesseebeelee per ee deezabeelee*
mobility problems	problemi di mobilità *problemee dee mobeeleeta*
blind people	non vedenti/ciechi *non vedentee/chee-ekee*
communication services for people with impaired hearing	servizi di comunicazione per i sordi/sordomuti/gli audiolesi *serveetsee dee komooneekatseeone per ee sordee/sordomootee/LYee aoodeoolezee*
Could you help me...?	Potrebbe aiutarmi...? *potrebbe aeeootarmee...?*
...to go up the stairs	...a salire le scale *a saleere le skale*
...to go down the stairs	...a scendere gli scalini *a shendere LYee skaleenee*
...to cross the road	...ad attraversare la strada *ad attraversare la strada*
Is there a ramp/a lift/a stair lift?	C'è una rampa/un ascensore/un montascale? *che oona rampa/oon ashensore/oon montaskale?*
There's something wrong with my wheelchair	La mia sedia a rotelle è guasta *la meea sedeea a rotelle e gooasta*
Does the theatre have facilities for disabled people?	Il teatro è accessibile ai disabili? *eel teatro e achchesseebeele aee deezabeelee?*
Do you have a toilet for disabled people?	C'è un bagno per i disabili? *che oon baNYo per ee deezabeelee?*

PROBLEMS AND QUESTIONS

Someone has taken my seat	Qualcuno ha occupato il mio posto *kooalkoono a okkoopato eel meeo posto*
I reserved the seat in London	Ho prenotato il posto a Londra *ho prenotato eel posto a londra*
I've missed my flight/train/boat	Ho perso l'aereo/il treno/la nave *ho perso laereo/eel treno/la nave*
I've missed my connection to...	Ho perso la coincidenza per... *o perso la koeencheedentsa per...*
Can I book a seat...?	Posso prenotare un posto...? *posso prenotare oon posto...?*
...on another flight	...su un altro volo *soo oon altro volo*
...on the next flight	...sul prossimo volo *sool prosseemo volo*
When does the next train for... leave?	Quando parte il prossimo treno per...? *kooando parte il prosseemo treno per...?*
Does the train stop at...?	Il treno si ferma a...? *eel treno see ferma a...?*
How long will the train stop at...?	Per quanto si ferma il treno a...? *per kooanto see ferma eel treno a...?*

SHOPPING AND SERVICES

Shopping reflects the rich variety of Italian products and lifestyles. It is an integral part of daily living. Italy has one of the highest ratios of shops per head of population in Europe.

The markets held in squares and streets offer a colourful and delicious range of fruits, vegetables and other agricultural produce as well as fashion and other household articles. Italy is famous for its fashion and design. Just look at the window displays of exclusive clothes shops.

Remember also that Italian craftsmanship has a long tradition of quality and style. Italian leather goods and glass are admired throughout the world. So there are plenty of possibilities for souvenirs.

Small shops are normally open from 8.30 or 9am to 12.30 or 1pm and from 3.30 or 4pm to 7.30 or 8pm. Most shops close at 1pm on Saturdays. Large hypermarkets and shopping centres are normally open from 9am to 9pm. Opening times vary from region to region as they are set by local byelaws.

TYPES OF SHOP

baker's	il panificio/la panetteria *eel paneefeecheeo/la panettereea*
bookshop (see section on Reading, page 67)	la libreria *la leebrereea*
boutique	la boutique/ il negozio d'abbigliamento *la booteek/ eel negotseeo dabbeeLYeeamento*
butcher's	la macelleria/il macellaio *la machellereea/eel machellaeeo*
cake and confectionary shop	la pasticceria *la pasteechchereea*
delicatessen shop	la salumeria/il salumiere *la saloomereea/eel saloomee-ere*
department stores	i grandi magazzini *ee grandee magadsdseenee*
do-it-yourself store	il negozio di bricolage/fai-da-te *eel negotseeo dee breekolaj/faee-da-te*
fishmonger's	la pescheria/il pescivendolo *la peskereea/eel pesheevendolo*

Small shops are normally open from 8.30 or 9am to 12.30 or 1pm and from 3.30 or 4pm to 7.30 or 8pm. Most shops close at 1pm on Saturdays. Large hypermarkets and shopping centres are normally open from 9am to 9pm. Opening times vary from region to region as they are set by local byelaws.

florist	il fioraio *eel feeoraeeo*
food shop	il negozio di generi alimentari *eel negotseeo dee jenere aleementaree*
greengrocer's	il negozio di frutta e verdura/ il verduraio/il fruttivendolo *eel negotseeo dee frootta e verdoora/ eel verdooraeeo/eel frooteevendolo*
grocer's	la drogheria *la drogereea*
haberdasher's	la merceria *la merchereea*
hardware shop	l'utensileria *lootenseelereea*
health food shop	l'erboristeria *lerboreestereea*
jeweller's	la gioielleria *la jeeoee-ellereea*
market	il mercato *eel merkato*
dairy	la latteria *la lattereea*
newsagent's	l'edicola/il giornalaio *ledeekola/eel jeeornalaeeo*
dispensing optician (see section in Health, page 81) and camera shop	l'ottico *lotteeko*
perfumery	la profumeria *la profoomereea*
petrol station (see Travel, page 92)	il distributore/il rifornitore *eel deestreebootore/eel reeforneetore*

pharmacy/chemist's (see Health section)	la farmacia *la farmacheea*
post office	l'ufficio postale *looffeecheeo postale*
shoe shop	la calzoleria *la kaltsolereea*
sports shop	il negozio di articoli sportivi *eel negotseeo dee arteekolee sporteevee*
stationer's	la cartoleria *la kartolereea*
supermarket/hypermarket	il supermercato/l'ipermercato *eel soopermerkato/leepermerkato*
shopping precinct/shopping centre	il centro commerciale *eel chentro kommercheeale*
tobacconist's	la tabaccheria *la tabakkereea*
travel agent	l'agenzia di viaggi *lajentseea dee veeajjee*
toy shop	il negozio di giocattoli *eel negotseeo dee jeeokattolee*
wine shop (selling high quality wine)	l'enoteca *lenoteka*
basket/trolley	il cestino/il carrello *eel chesteeno/eel karrello*
I'd like to buy this	Vorrei comprare questo *vorre-ee komprare kooesto*
customer	il/la cliente *eel/la klee-ente*
expensive	caro *karo*
cheap	a buon prezzo/a buon mercato *a boo-on pretstso/ a boo-on merkato*

hire purchase	l'acquisto a rate *lakkooeesto a rate*
sale/for sale	la vendita/in vendita *la vendeeta/een vendeeta*
self-service	il negozio self-service *eel negotseeo self-servees*
Do you sell...?	Vende...? *vende...?*

You may see:

Liquidazione totale	Everything must go
Saldi/Svendita/Liquidazione	Clearance sale
Con uno sconto del cinquanta per cento	Half price
Gratis	Absolutely free
Grandi occasioni	Great bargains
Prezzi eccezionali	Exceptional prices
Omaggio	Free gift

shop assistant	il commesso/la commessa *eel kommesso/la kommessa*
show window	la vetrina *la vetreena*
Can I help you?	Desidera? *dezeedera?*
I'd like to see/buy...	Vorrei vedere/comprare... *vorre-ee vedere/komprare...*
I'm looking for...	Cerco... *cherko...*
I'm just looking	Sto solo dando uno sguardo *sto solo dando oono zgooardo*
Which makes do you sell...?	Che marche vendete...? *ke marke vendete...?*

When will you have...?	Quando avrete...? *kooando avrete...?*
Where could I find some...?	Dove potrei trovare...? *dove potre-ee trovare...?*
I'd like three...	Vorrei tre... *vorre-ee tre...*

SUPERMARKETS AND FOOD SHOPS

Italian bread is sold by the kilo and comes in a variety of shapes and sizes.

a kilo of...	un chilo di... *oon keelo dee...*
half a kilo of...	mezzo chilo di... *medsdso keelo dee...*
a hectogram (100g) of...	un etto di... *oon etto dee...*
a litre of...	un litro di... *oon leetro dee...*
two boxes of...	due scatole di... *dooe skatole dee...*
one bottle...	una bottiglia... *oona botteeLYeea...*
a two-litre bottle...	un bottiglione... *oon botteeLYeeone...*
a container...	un contenitore... *oon konteneetore...*
a packet...	un pacco... *oon pakko...*
a tube...	un tubetto... *oon toobetto...*
a tin...	un barattolo... *oon barattolo...*

a small tin...	una scatoletta... *oona skatoletta...*
white bread/wholemeal bread	il pane bianco/il pane integrale *eel pane beeanko/eel pane eentegrale*
bread roll/bread stick	il panino, la pagnotta/il filoncino *eel paneeno, la paNYotta/ eel feeloncheeno*
sandwich loaf	il pane in cassetta *eel pane een kassetta*
sliced sandwich loaf	il pancarrè *eel pankarre*
butter/margarine	il burro/la margarina *eel boorro/la margareena*
coffee/ground coffee/ coffee beans	il caffè/il caffè macinato/ i chicchi di caffè *eel kaffe/eel kaffe macheenato /ee keekee dee kaffe*
flour	la farina *la fareena*
pasta/spaghetti/rice	la pasta/gli spaghetti/il riso *la pasta/LYee spagettee/eel reezo*
sugar	lo zucchero *lo dsookkero*
paper napkins/paper tissues	i tovaglioli di carta/ i fazzoletti di carta *ee tovaLYeeoleenee dee karta/ ee fatstsolettee dee karta*
toilet paper	la carta igienica *la karta eejee-eneeka*
washing powder	il detersivo *eel deterseevo*
washing-up liquid	il detersivo per i piatti *eel deterseevo per ee peeattee*

baby food	gli omogeneizzati *LYee omojene-eedsdsatee*
disposable nappies	i pannolini per bambini *ee pannoleenee per bambeenee*
I'd like eight bread rolls	Mi dia otto panini *mee deea otto paneenee*
I'd like two kilograms of bread	Due chili di pane per favore *dooe keelee dee pane per favore*

DELICATESSENS AND CHEESE SHOPS

fresh/mature cheese	il formaggio fresco/stagionato *eel formajjeeo fresko/stajeeonato*
grated cheese	il formaggio grattugiato *eel formajjeeo grattoojeeato*
raw/cooked ham	il prosciutto crudo/cotto *eel prosheeootto kroodo/kotto*
fresh/long life milk	il latte fresco/ a lunga conservazione *eel latte fresko/ a loonga konservatseeone*
whole/semi-skimmed/ skimmed milk	il latte intero/parzialmente scremato/scremato *eel latte eentero/partseealmente skremato/skremato*
I'd like some sliced items	Vorrei un po' di affettati *vorre-ee oon po dee affettatee*
I'd like to taste that ham	Vorrei assaggiare quel prosciutto *vorre-ee assajjeeare kooel prosheeootto*

BUTCHER'S

See Eating Out section.

beef	la carne bovina, il manzo *la karne boveena, eel manzo*
goat/kid	la carne caprina *la karne kapreena*
horse meat	la carne equina, la carne di cavallo *la karne ekooeena, la karne dee kavallo*
lamb/mutton	la carne ovina, la carne di agnello *la karne oveena, la karne dee aNYello*
pork	la carne suina, la carne di maiale *la karne sooeena, la karne dee maeeale*
poultry	il pollame *eel pollame*
game	la selvaggina *la selvajjeena*
mince	la carne macinata/la carne tritata *la karne macheenata/la karne treetata*
tripe	la trippa *la treeppa*
I'd like some very lean meat	Vorrei della carne magrissima *vorre-ee della karne magreesseema*
That steak has too much fat	Quella bistecca ha troppo grasso *kooella beestekka a troppo grasso*
One kilo of stewing beef	Un chilo di manzo per fare uno spezzatino *oon keelo dee mandso per fare oono spetstsateeno*

FISHMONGER'S

See **Eating Out** *section.*

fresh fish	il pesce fresco *eel peshe fresko*
frozen fish	il pesce surgelato *eel peshe soorjelato*
shellfish	i crostacei *ee krostache-ee*
Half a kilo of sardines	Mezzo chilo di sardine *medsdso keelo dee sardeene*
Could you gut the fish for me?	Me lo pulisce per favore? *me lo pooleeshe per favore?*

DEPARTMENT STORE

On which floor are the domestic appliances?	A che piano sono gli elettrodomestici? *a ke peeano sono LYee elettrodomesteechee?*
Where is the gift department?	Dove sono gli articoli da regalo? *dove sono LYee arteekolee da regalo?*
escalator	la scala mobile *la skala mobeele*
floor	il piano *eel peeano*
lifts	gli ascensori *LYee ashensoree*
stairs	le scale *le skale*

For sizes of clothes and shoes see section in **Appendix, pages 130 - 131.**

CLOTHING

For sizes of clothes and shoes see section in **Appendix, pages 130 -131.**

size	la taglia *la taLYeea*
shoe size	il numero di scarpa *eel noomero dee skarpa*
designer clothes	gli abiti firmati *LYee abeetee feermatee*
anorak	la giacca a vento *la jeeakka a vento*
coat	il cappotto *eel kappotto*
gloves	i guanti *ee gooantee*
hat/cap	il cappello/il berretto *eel kappello/eel berretto*
headscarf	il foulard *eel foolar*
jacket	la giacca *la jeeakka*
shorts	i pantaloncini corti *ee pantaloncheenee kortee*
short/long skirt	la gonna corta/lunga *la gonna korta/loonga*
socks/stockings	le calze *le kaltse*
suit (male)	l'abito *labeeto*
suit (female)	il tailleur *eel taee-er*
tie	la cravatta *la kravatta*

tights	i collant *ee kollant*
trousers	i pantaloni/i calzoni *ee pantalonee/ee kaltsonee*
underwear	la biancheria intima *la beeankereea eenteema*
bra	il reggiseno *eel rejjeeseno*
I'd like to try it on	Vorrei provarlo *vorre-ee provarlo*
This feels tight. Can I try a bigger size?	È troppo stretto. Potrei provare una taglia più grande? *e troppo stretto. potre-ee provare oona taLYeea peeoo grande?*
I wear size 18 clothes and size 6 shoes	Ho la taglia quarantaquattro e calzo il trentanove *o la taLYeea kooarantakooattro e kaltso eel trentanove*

HABERDASHER'S

zip	la cerniera *la chernee-era*
button	il bottone *eel bottone*
material	il tessuto/la stoffa *eel tessooto/la stoffa*
lining	la fodera *la fodera*
needle	l'ago *lago*
thread	il filo per cucire *eel feelo per koocheere*
one metre	un metro *oon metro*

two metres	due metri *dooe metree*
I'd like two and a half metres of this material	Vorrei due metri e mezzo di questa stoffa *vorre-ee dooe metree e medsdso dee kooestsa stoffa*
How much is a metre of this material?	Quant'è al metro questa stoffa? *kooante al metro kooesta stoffa?*
bed linen (sheets/pillowcases)	la biancheria da letto (lenzuola/federe) *la beeankereea da letto (lentsoo-ola/federe)*
table linen (cloths/serviettes)	la biancheria da tavola (tovaglie/tovaglioli) *la beeankereea da tavola (tovaLYee-e/tovaLYeeolee)*
towels/tea towels	gli asciugamani/gli strofinacci *LYee asheeoogamanee/LYee strofeenachchee*

TOILETRIES AND COSMETICS

after-shave lotion	il dopobarba *eel dopobarba*
deodorant	il deodorante *eel deodorante*
face cream	la crema per il viso *la krema per eel veezo*
hair gel/hair mousse	il gel/la spuma *eel gel/la spooma*
make-up	il trucco *eel trookko*
nail varnish/nail varnish remover	lo smalto per unghie/l'acetone *lo zmalto per oongee-e/lachetone*

perfume	il profumo *eel profoomo*
shampoo for greasy/dry/normal hair	lo shampoo per capelli grassi/secchi/normali *lo shampo per kapellee grassee/sekkee/normalee*
shaving foam	la schiuma da barba *la skeeooma da barba*
soap	il sapone/la saponetta *eel sapone/la saponetta*
fluoride toothpaste	il dentifricio al fluoro *eel denteefreecheeo al floo-oro*
I'd like a non-allergenic cream	Vorrei una crema anti-allergica *vorre-ee oona krema antee allerjeeka*
Do you sell products for sensitive skins?	Vende prodotti per pelli delicate? *vende prodottee per pellee deleekate?*

TOBACCONIST'S

cigar	il sigaro *eel seegaro*
cigarette	la sigaretta *la seegaretta*
cigarette lighter	l'accendino *lachchendeeno*
matches	i fiammiferi/i cerini *ee feeammeeferee/ee chereenee*
pipe	la pipa *la peepa*
postcard	la cartolina *la kartoleena*
tobacco	il tabacco *eel tabakko*

two packets of 20 cigarettes	due pacchetti da 20 sigarette *dooe pakkettee da ventee seegarette*
How much are these postcards?	Quanto costano queste cartoline? *kooanto kostano kooeste kartoleene?*
Can I have the stamps for them as well?	Mi dà anche i francobolli per queste? *mee da anke ee frankobollee per kooeste?*
A box of matches please	Una scatola di cerini per favore *oona skatola dee chereenee per favore*
Do you have any English/American cigarettes?	Avete sigarette inglesi/americane? *avete seegarette eenglezee/amereekane?*

STATIONER'S

adhesive tape	il nastro adesivo/lo scotch *eel nastro adezeevo/lo skoch*
biro	la penna biro *la penna beero*
birthday card	il biglietto d'auguri di compleanno *eel beeLYee-etto daoogooree dee kompleanno*
calculator	la calcolatrice *la kalkolatreeche*
eraser	la gomma per cancellare *la gomma per kanchellare*
envelope	la busta *la boosta*
greetings card	il biglietto d'auguri *eel beeLYee-etto daoogooree*

map	la carta geografica/la mappa *la karta jeografeeka/la mappa*
pen/felt-tip/fountain pen	la penna/il pennarello/ la stilografica *la penna/eel pennarello/ la steelografeeka*
pencil	la matita/il lapis *la mateeta/eel lapees*
pencil sharpener	il temperamatite/il temperalapis *eel temperamateete/eel temperalapees*
ream of paper	la risma di carta *la reezma dee karta*
staple/stapler	la graffetta/la cucitrice *la graffetta/la koocheetreeche*
writing paper	la carta da lettere *la karta da lettere*

WRAPPING AND PAYING

carrier bag/shopping bag	la busta/la borsa *la boosta/la borsa*
cashier	la cassiera/il cassiere *la kassee-era/eel kassee-ere*
change	il resto *eel resto*
queue/do I queue here?	la fila, la coda/faccio la fila qui? *la feela, la koda/fachcheeo la feela kooee?*
receipt	lo scontrino *lo skontreeno*
Where can I pay?	dov'è la cassa? *dove la kassa?*
How much is it?/ How much are they?	Quanto costa?/Quanto costano? *kooanto kosta?/kooanto kostano?*

It's more than I thought	È più di quanto pensassi *e peeoo dee kooanto pensassee*
What discount can you give me?	Che sconto mi fa? *ke skonto mee fa?*
If I buy three will you give me a better price?	Se ne compro tre mi fa un prezzo migliore? *se ne kompro tre mee fa oon pretstso meeLYeeore?*
I can't afford it	Non me lo posso permettere *non me lo posso permettere*
Could you giftwrap it for me?	Mi fa una confezione regalo? *mee fa oona konfetseeone regalo?*
Could I have a carrier bag?	Mi dà una busta per favore? *mee da oona boosta per favore?*

APPENDIX

COMMON ABBREVIATIONS USED IN ITALY

ACI	Automobile Club Italiano	Italian Automobile Association
BI	Banca d'Italia	Bank of Italy
C	Celsius, Centigrado	Celsius, Centigrade
ca	corrente anno (in correspondence)	Of the present year
CA	Per la Cortese Attenzione	For the kind attention of
c/c	conto corrente	Current account
CC	Carabinieri	Carabinieri Police Force
CC	Camera di Commercio	Chamber of Commerce
CIT	Compagnia Italiana Turismo	Italian Tourist Agency
CV	Cavallo Vapore	Horsepower
Dott Dr	Dottore	Medical Doctor/ University graduate (male)
Dott.ssa	Dottoressa	Medical Doctor/University graduate (female)
Dott Ing	Dottore Ingegnere	Engineering Graduate
ENEL	Ente Nazionale per l'Energia Elettrica	National Electricity Board
ENIT	Ente Nazionale Italiano per il Turismo	State Tourist Board
UE	Unione Europea	European Union
FS	Ferrovie dello Stato	State Railway

G.d.F	Guardia di Finanza	Customs and Excise Police
IVA	Imposta Valore Aggiunto	Value Added Tax (VAT)
ONU	Organizzazione Nazioni Unite	United Nations Organisation
PPTT	Poste e Telecomunicazioni	Post Office
PS	Pubblica Sicurezza	State Police
RAI	Radio Televisione Italiana	Italian Broadcasting Corporation
Sig.	Signor (followed by surname)	Mr
Sig.ra	Signora (followed by surname)	Mrs
Sig.na	Signorina (followed by surname)	Miss
SIP	Società Italiana per l'Esercizio delle Telecomunicazioni	Italian Telecom
TCI	Touring Club Italiano	Italian organisation like the AA

DAYS OF THE WEEK

Monday	lunedì *loonedee*
Tuesday	martedì *martedee*
Wednesday	mercoledì *merkoledee*
Thursday	giovedì *jeeovedee*
Friday	venerdì *venerdee*
Saturday	sabato *sabato*
Sunday	domenica *domeneeka*

SEASONS

spring	la primavera *la preemavera*
summer	l'estate *lestate*
autumn	l'autunno *laootoonno*
winter	l'inverno *leenverno*

MONTHS

January	gennaio *jennaeeo*
February	febbraio *febbraeeo*
March	marzo *martso*
April	aprile *apreele*
May	maggio *majjeeo*
June	giugno *jeeooNYo*
July	luglio *looLYeeo*
August	agosto *agosto*
September	settembre *settembre*
October	ottobre *ottobre*

November	novembre *novembre*
December	dicembre *deechembre*

ITALIAN NATIONAL HOLIDAYS

New Year's Day (1st January)	Capodanno, Primo dell'anno
Epiphany (6th January)	Epifania
Easter	Pasqua
Easter Monday	Pasquetta, Lunedì di Pasqua
Liberation Day (25th April)	Anniversario della Liberazione
Labour Day (1st May)	Festa del lavoro, il Primo Maggio
Assumption Day (15th August)	Ferragosto
All Saints' Day (1st November)	Tutti i Santi
Immaculate Conception (8th December)	Immacolata
Christmas Day (25th December)	Natale
Boxing Day (26th December)	Santo Stefano

DISTANCES BETWEEN MAJOR CITIES (KM)

	Bologna	Brindisi	Firenze	Genova	Milano	Napoli	Reggio Calabria	Roma	Torino	Trieste
Brindisi	780									
Firenze	105	835								
Genova	295	1060	225							
Milano	210	990	300	140						
Napoli	590	375	490	715	785					
Reggio Calabria	1080	455	975	1200	1270	500				
Roma	380	565	275	500	570	220	705			
Torino	330	1110	395	170	140	880	1370	670		
Trieste	295	1015	395	540	410	880	1370	670	545	
Venezia	150	875	255	400	265	740	1225	530	400	160

CONVERSION TABLES

DISTANCE

E.g. 10 km = 6 miles, 10 miles = 16 km

miles	6	12	19	25	31	37	44	50	56	62	68	75	81
km/miles	10	20	30	40	50	60	70	80	90	100	110	120	130
km	16	32	48	64	80	97	113	129	145	161	177	194	210

TEMPERATURE

°F	0	20	32	50	70	87	98.6	104	212
°C	-18	-7	0	10	21	31	37	40	100

LIQUIDS

litres	5	10	15	20	25	30	35	40	45	50
imperial gallons	1.1	2.2	3.3	4.4	5.5	6.6	7.7	8.8	9.9	11.0
US gallons	1.3	2.6	3.9	5.2	6.5	7.8	9.1	10.4	11.7	13.0

WEIGHTS

E.g. 1kg = 2.2lbs, 1lb = 0.46kg

lbs	1.1	2.2	4.4	6.6	8.8	11.0	13.2	15.4	17.6	19.8	21.0
kg/lbs	0.5	1	2	3	4	5	6	7	8	9	10
kg	0.23	0.46	0.92	1.38	1.84	2.3	2.76	3.22	3.68	4.14	4.6

NB 1000g = 1kg

MATERIALS

cotton	il cotone *eel kotone*
wool	la lana *la lana*
silk	la seta *la seta*
velvet	il velluto *eel vellooto*
leather	la pelle, il cuoio *la pelle, eel koo-o-eeo*
lace	il pizzo *eel peetstso*

CLOTHES SIZES

Men's suits

British	36	38	40	42	44	46	48	50
American	36	38	40	42	44	46	48	50
Continental	46	48	50/52	54	56	58/60	62	64

Men's shirts

British	14	14½	15	15½	16	16½	17	17½
American	14	14½	15	15½	16	16½	17	17½
Continental	35	36/37	38	39/40	41	42/43	44	45

Men's shoes

British	7	7½	8	8½	9	9½	10	10½	11
American	7½	8	8½	9	9½	10	10½	11	11½
Continental	41		42		43		44		45

Women's sizes

British	8	10	12	14	16	18	20	22
American	-	8	10	12	14	16	18	20
Continental	-	36	38	40	42	44	46	48

Women's shoes

British	4	4½	5	5½	6	6½	7	7½
American	5½	6	6½	7	7½	8	8½	9
Continental	36	37	38	38	39	40	41	41

COLOURS

black — nero
nero

red — rosso
rosso

yellow — giallo
jeeallo

brown — marrone
marrone

white — bianco
beeanko

blue — blu
bloo

green — verde
verde

grey — grigio
greejeeo

USEFUL ADDRESSES IN THE UK

Alitalia

4, Portman Square,
London W1H 6LD
Tel: +44 (0)208 745 8200
www.alitalia.co.uk

Italian Chamber of Commerce
and Industry for the UK

1, Princes Street
London W1B 2AY
Tel: +44 (0)207 495 8191
www.italchamind.org.uk

Italian Consulate

38, Eaton Place
London
SW1X 8AN
Tel: +44 (0)207 2359371
Fax: +44 (0)207 8231609
www.embitaly.org.uk

Italian Embassy

14, Three Kings' Yard
London W1Y 2EH
Tel: +44 (0)207 3122200
Fax: +44 (0)207 4992283
E-mail: emblondon@embitaly.org.uk
www.embitaly.org.uk

Italian Cultural Institute

39, Belgrave Square
London SW1X 8NX
Tel: +44 (0)207 235 1461
Fax: +44 (0)207 235 4618
E-mail: ici@italcultur.org.uk
www.italcultur.org.uk/

Italian State Tourist Office (ENIT)	1, Princes Street London W1R 2AY Tel: +44 (0)207 408 1254 Fax: +44 (0)207 3993567 E-mail: Enitlond@globalnet.co.uk www.enit.it/enit2/
Italian Trade Centre	37, Sackville Street London W1X 2DQ Tel: +44 (0) 207 734 2412 Fax: +44 (0) 207 734 2516 www.ice.it/estero/londra/

EMBASSIES AND CONSULATES

UNITED KINGDOM

Rome - Roma	Via XX Settembre 80a I-00187 Roma RM Tel: +39 06 4220 0001 E-mail: info@rome.mail.fco.gov.uk Website: www.UkinItalia.it
Milan – Milano	Via San Paolo 7 I-20121 Milano MI Tel: +39 02 72300 Fax: +39 02 8692405
Venice – Venezia	Accademia Dorsoduro, 1051 30123 Venezia VE Tel: +39 041 5227207 Fax: +39 041 5522617

Florence - Firenze

Lungarno Corsini 2
I-50123 Firenze FI
Tel:+39 055 284133
Fax:+39 055 219112
e-mail: bcflocom@tin.it

UNITED STATES

Rome – Roma

Via Vittorio Veneto 119/A
00187 Roma
Tel: +39 06 46741
Fax: +39 06 4882672
or 06 4674 2356
http://www.usembassy.it/mission/

Milan – Milano

Via Princ. Amedeo 2/10
20121 Milan
Tel:+39 02 290351
Fax:+39 02 2900 1165
http://www.usembassy.it/milan/

Florence - Firenze

Lungarno Vespucci 38
50123, Firenze
Tel:+39 055 2398 276
Fax:+39 055 284 088
http://www.usembassy.it/florence/

Naples - Napoli

Piazza della Repubblica
80122 Napoli
Tel:+39 081 583811
Fax:+39 081 7611869
http://www.usembassy.it/naples/

Palermo

Via Vaccarini 1
Tel:+39 091 305 857
Fax:+39 091 625 6026
http://www.usembassy.it/palermo/

ITALIAN AIRPORTS

Rome	Leonardo da Vinci – Fiumicino	Tel. 06 659 53640
	Ciampino	Tel. 06 794941
Milan	Linate	Tel. 02 748 5 2200
	Malpensa	Tel. 02 748 5 2200
Turin	Caselle	Tel. 011 5676361
Genoa	Cristoforo Colombo	Tel. 010 6015410
Venice	Marco Polo	Tel. 041 2606111/ 2381590
Bologna	Guglielmo Marconi	Tel. 051 6479615
Florence	Amerigo Vespucci	Tel. 055 373498
Pisa	Galileo Galilei	Tel. 050 849402
Naples	Capodichino	Tel. 081 7896259
Cagliari	Mario Marmelidi di Elmas	Tel. 070 212076/9
Palermo	Punta Raisi	Tel. 091 591690/ 591275

TELEPHONING ABROAD FROM ITALY

United Kingdom	0044, then STD code without the initial 0
London	0044 207/208
Cardiff	0044 2920
Belfast	0044 2890
Edinburgh	0044 131
Dublin	003531
USA/Canada	001
Washington DC	00 1 202
New York City	00 1 718
San Francisco	00 1 415

USEFUL TELEPHONE NUMBERS

Emergency services (Carabinieri)	112	Pronto intervento
Emergency services (Police)	113	Pronto intervento
Early morning calls	114	Sveglia
Fire station	115	Vigili del fuoco
Breakdown recovery	116	Soccorso stradale A.C.I.
Customs and excise	117	Guardia di finanza
Paramedics	118	Pronto intervento medico
Snow report	162	Notiziario della neve
Weather forecast	191	Previsioni metereologiche
Road report	194	Percorribilità strade
Duty chemists	192	Farmacie di turno

SIGNS AND NOTICES

Affittasi	To let/For hire
Al completo	Full/No vacancies
Alt	Stop
Aperto	Open
Attenti al cane	Beware of the dog
Attenzione	Caution
Caldo	Hot
Cassa	Cash desk
Chiuso	Closed
Divieto di sosta	No parking
Donne	Ladies
Entrata	Entrance

Fermata	Bus stop
Freddo	Cold
Fuori servizio	Out of order
Libero	Vacant
Non disturbare	Do not disturb
Non toccare	Do not touch
Occupato	Occupied/Engaged
Pericolo	Danger
Pittura/Vernice fresca	Wet paint
Privato	Private
Proprietà privata	Private property
Riservato	Reserved
Senso unico	One way
Spingere	Push
Strada privata	Private road
Svendite	Sales
Tirare	Pull
Transito con catene	Chains required
Uomini	Gentlemen
Uscita (di sicurezza)	(Emergency) exit
Veleno	Poison
Vendesi	For sale
Vietato fumare	No smoking
Vietato l'accesso	No entry
Vietato l'ingresso	No entrance
Vietato sputare	Do not spit
Vietato toccare	Do not touch

DICTIONARY

Both masculine and feminine forms are given for adjectives
e.g. Italian: italiano/a = italiano (m)/italiana (f).

A
above sopra/su
abroad all'estero
to accept accettare
to accompany accompagnare
ache il dolore
address l'indirizzo
adult l'adulto/a
to advise consigliare
aeroplane l'aeroplano
after dopo
afternoon il pomeriggio
age l'età
agent l'agente
air l'aria
  air hostess l'hostess
  airline la compagnia aerea
  airport l'aeroporto
alarm clock la sveglia
all tutto/a
almost quasi
Alps le Alpi
already già
also anche
always sempre
ambulance l'ambulanza
American americano/a
amusing divertente
and e
animal l'animale

ankle la caviglia
anniversary l'anniversario
antique antico/a
antiques dealer l'antiquario
apartment l'appartamento
aperitif l'aperitivo
appearance l'aspetto
appetite l'appetito
apple la mela
apricot l'albicocca
April aprile
arch l'arco
architect l'architetto
arm il braccio
around intorno/attorno
to arrive arrivare
art l'arte
artichoke il carciofo
article l'articolo
artist l'artista
to ask chiedere/domandare
asparagus gli asparagi
assistant l'assistente
aubergine la melanzana
August agosto
aunt la zia
Australia l'Australia
Austria l'Austria
autumn l'autunno
avenue il viale

average la media

B
baby il bambino/la bambina
back (body) la schiena
bacon il bacon/
la pancetta affumicata
badly male
bag la borsa
baker's la panetteria/il
panificio
balcony il balcone
ball la palla/il pallone
banana la banana
band la banda
bank la banca
bank (of river) la riva
banquet il banchetto
bar il bar
barber il barbiere
basil il basilico
basilica la basilica
basin la bacinella
basket il cestino
bath il bagno
bath tub la vasca da bagno
to bathe fare il bagno
bathing costume il costume
da bagno
bathroom la stanza da bagno/
il bagno
battery la batteria/la pila
to be essere
to be able potere
to be called chiamarsi
to be enough/suffice bastare

beach la spiaggia
beans i fagioli
beard la barba
beautiful bello/a
to become diventare
bed il letto
bedroom la camera/
la stanza da letto
bedspread il copriletto
bee l'ape
beef il manzo
beer la birra
beginning l'inizio
behind dietro
to believe credere
bell la campana
to belong appartenere
belt la cintura/il cinto
bench la panchina
better meglio/migliore
beware! attenzione!
bicycle la bicicletta
big grande, grosso/a
bill il conto
bird l'uccello
birth la nascita
birthday il compleanno
biscuit il biscotto
bitter amaro/a
black nero/a
blanket la coperta
blonde biondo/a
blouse la camicetta
blue azzurro/a, celeste, blu
boarding house la pensione
boat la barca

body il corpo
to boil bollire
bone l'osso
bonnet (car) il cofano
book il libro
to book prenotare
booking la prenotazione
bookseller il libraio
bookshop la libreria
bookstall l'edicola
boot (shoe) lo stivale
  (of car) il portabagagli
born nato/a
to borrow prendere in prestito
bottle la bottiglia
  bottle opener il cavatappi/
  l'apribottiglie
  bottle top il tappo
bottom (e.g. sea) il fondo
bottom (body) il sedere
bowl la ciotola
box la scatola
boy il ragazzo
brake il freno
to brake frenare
bread il pane
  bread roll il panino/
  la pagnotta
to break rompere
breakfast la (prima) colazione
to have breakfast fare
  colazione
to breathe respirare
bride la sposa
bridegroom lo sposo
bridge il ponte

brief breve
briefcase la ventiquattore/
  la diplomatica
briefs lo slip
broken rotto/a
brother il fratello
brother-in-law il cognato
brown marrone
brush il pennello/
  la spazzola
to brush spazzolare
to brush one's teeth lavarsi i
  denti
to build costruire
building l'edificio/il palazzo
bunch (keys/flowers) il mazzo
bunch (of grapes) il grappolo
bus l'autobus/il bus
business gli affari
but ma/però
butcher's la macelleria
butter il burro
butterfly la farfalla
button il bottone
to buy comprare/acquistare
  to buy a ticket fare il
  biglietto
bye! ciao!

C

cabbage il cavolo/la verza
café il caffè/il bar
cake il dolce/la torta
calculator la calcolatrice
calendar il calendario
calf il vitello

to call chiamare
camera la macchina fotografica
camping il campeggio
campsite il campeggio
can il barattolo/la lattina
Canada il Canada
canal il canale
to cancel cancellare
candle la candela
canoe la canoa
canoeing il canottaggio
capital il/la capitale
car la macchina/l'auto(mobile)
   car driver l'automobilista
   car park il parcheggio/
   il posteggio
carafe la caraffa
caravan la roulotte/il caravan
carbonated gassato/a
care la cura
carpet il tappeto
carriage la carrozza/il vagone
carrot la carota
to carry portare
cash register il registratore di
   cassa
castle il castello
cat il gatto
cathedral la cattedrale
cauliflower il cavolfiore
to cause causare
cave la grotta
CD, CD player il CD, il lettore
   di CD
to cease smettere
ceiling il soffitto

to celebrate festeggiare
celery il sedano
cellar la cantina
cemetery il cimitero/
   il camposanto
centre il centro
century il secolo
ceramics la ceramica
certain certo/a
chair la sedia
change (money) il resto
   (small) gli spiccioli/la moneta
to change cambiare
channel il canale
Channel (the English) la Manica
Channel Tunnel il tunnel della
   Manica
chapel la cappella
to chat chiacchierare
   (on the Net) chattare
check il controllo
check-out assistant il cassiere/
   la cassiera
cheek la guancia
cheerful allegro/a
cheese il formaggio
chemist's la farmacia
cheque l'assegno
cherry la ciliegia
chest (body) il petto
chicken il pollo
chin il mento
chocolate il cioccolato
   (hot) la cioccolata
Christmas il Natale
church la chiesa

cigar il sigaro
cigarette la sigaretta
cinema il cinema
circle il cerchio/il circolo
circuit il giro/il circuito
circus il circo
city la città
clam la vongola
class la classe
classroom l'aula
clean pulito/a
to clean pulire
cleaner's la lavanderia
clear chiaro/a
clerk l'impiegato/a
client il/la cliente
to close chiudere
closed chiuso/a
cloth la stoffa
clothes i vestiti
  clothes hanger l'attaccapanni
clothing l'abbigliamento
cloud la nuvola
coach il pullman/la corriera
coat il cappotto
coconut la noce di cocco
coffee il caffè
  coffee pot la caffettiera
coin la moneta
colander il colapasta
cold freddo/a (adj),
  il raffreddore (noun)
collapse il crollo
colleague il/la collega
college il collegio
colour il colore

comb il pettine
to come venire
comic il giornalino
comics i fumetti
commerce il commercio
to communicate comunicare
companion il compagno/la
  compagna
company la compagnia
  (firm) l'azienda/la società/
  la ditta
to comprise comprendere
computer il computer
concert il concerto
conductor (orchestra) il
  direttore d'orchestra
conference il congresso
confusion la confusione
congratulations gli auguri
congratulations! complimenti!
to contain contenere
cook il cuoco/la cuoca
to cook cucinare
cork il tappo di sughero
corn il grano
cost il costo
to cost costare
cot la culla/il lettino
cotton il cotone
to count contare
counter (shop) il banco
country il paese/la nazione
countryside la campagna
couple la coppia
courgette la zucchina/
  lo zucchino

courtyard il cortile
cousin il cugino/la cugina
cow la mucca
crab il granchio
craftsman l'artigiano
crane la gru
cream la panna
to create creare
cricket (animal) il grillo
  (game) il cricket
crockery le stoviglie
to cross attraversare
crossroads l'incrocio
crowd la folla
to cry piangere/gridare
cucumber il cetriolo
cup la tazza/scodella
cupboard la credenza
current (present) attuale
  (river) la corrente
curtain la tenda
cushion il cuscino
custom il costume/l'usanza
customs la dogana
to cut tagliare
cutlery le posate
cutlet la cotoletta

D
daddy il babbo/papà
daily (newspaper) il quotidiano/
  il giornale
to dance ballare/danzare
danger il pericolo
dangerous pericoloso/a
dark scuro/a

daughter la figlia
day il giorno/la giornata
  day after tomorrow
  dopodomani
dead morto/a
deaf sordo/a
dear caro/a
December dicembre
to decide decidere
deer il cervo
delay il ritardo
to delete cancellare
delicate delicato/a
delicatessen's la salumeria
delicious squisito/a
dentist il/la dentista
department il reparto
to describe descrivere
design il disegno
to desire desiderare
detergent il detersivo
to develop sviluppare/
  svilupparsi
development lo sviluppo
dictionary il vocabolario/
  il dizionario
to die morire
diesel il diesel/il gasolio
different diverso/a, differente
difficult difficile
to digest digerire
digital camera la fotocamera
  digitale
dining room la sala da pranzo
dinner la cena
direction la direzione

director il/la direttore/trice
directory (telephone) l'elenco
dirty sporco/a
disabled (the) i disabili
disagreeable antipatico/a
discount lo sconto
to discuss discutere
dishwasher la lavastoviglie
disk il disco
distant lontano/a
to dive in tuffarsi
divorced divorziato/a
to do fare
doctor il dottore/il medico
document il documento
dog il cane
dollar il dollaro
donkey l'asino
door la porta
door bell il campanello
double doppio/a
doubt il dubbio
dove la colomba
down giù
downpour l'acquazzone
drawer il cassetto
dress l'abito/il vestito
to dress vestire/vestirsi
dressed vestito/a
dressing gown la vestaglia/
   la veste da camera
drink la bevanda/la bibita
to drink bere
to drive guidare
driver l'autista/il conducente
drop la goccia

drugs la droga
drunk ubriaco/a
dry asciutto/a, secco/a
duck l'anatra
dust la polvere
dustbin la pattumiera

E
each ogni/ciascuno
ear l'orecchio
early presto/di buon'ora
to earn guadagnare
earth la terra
east l'est
Easter la Pasqua
easy facile/semplice
to eat mangiare
e-commerce il commercio
   elettronico
economy l'economia
editor il redattore
egg l'uovo
eiderdown il piumino
eight otto
elbow il gomito
electric cooker la cucina
   elettrica
elegant elegante
e-mail (a message) una email
e-mail address l'indirizzo di
   posta elettronica
to embrace abbracciare
empty vuoto/a
end la fine/il termine
England l'Inghilterra
English inglese

to enjoy oneself divertirsi
enormous enorme, immenso/a
enough abbastanza
entrance l'entrata/l'ingresso
environment l'ambiente
equal uguale
Euro l'Euro
Europe l'Europa
European europeo/a
European Union l'Unione
  Europea
evening la sera
every ogni
exact esatto/a
exactly appunto
examination l'esame
example l'esempio
except escluso/tranne/eccetto
exchange rate il tasso di
  cambio
exercise l'esercizio
exhibition la mostra/
  l'esposizione
experience l'esperienza
expert l'esperto/il perito
to explain spiegare
exterior l'esterno
to extinguish spegnere
extinguisher l'estintore
eye l'occhio
eyebrows le sopracciglia

F
face la faccia
factory la fabbrica
to fall cadere

family la famiglia
far lontano/a
farm la fattoria
farmer l'agricoltore
fascinating affascinante
fashion la moda
fast veloce, rapido/a
  fast train il diretto
fat grasso/a
father il padre
favour il favore
fax il fax
  fax number il numero di fax
February febbraio
to feel sentire/sentirsi
female/feminine femminile
ferry boat il traghetto
few pochi/e, alcuni/e
fiancé il fidanzato
fiancée la fidanzata
field il campo
to fill up fare benzina
film il film
to find trovare
fine (penalty) la multa/
  la contravvenzione
  (eg weather) bello/a
finger il dito della mano
to finish finire/terminare
fire il fuoco
fireman il pompiere/
  il vigile del fuoco
first primo/a
fish il pesce
to fish pescare
fisherman il pescatore

fishing la pesca
  fishing rod la canna da pesca
five cinque
flag la bandiera
flea la pulce
to flee fuggire
flight il volo
floor il pavimento
florist il fiorista/il fioraio
flour la farina
flower il fiore
flute il flauto
fly la mosca
to fly volare
fog la nebbia
to follow seguire
food il cibo
foot il piede
forbidden vietato/a
forehead la fronte
foreign straniero/a
foreigner lo/la straniero/a
forest la foresta
to forget dimenticare
fork la forchetta
fountain la fontana
France la Francia
free (no charge) gratis,
  gratuito/a
  (not occupied) libero/a
freezer il congelatore/il freezer
French francese
  French beans i fagiolini
frequent frequente
fresh fresco/a
Friday venerdì

friend l'amico/a
friendship l'amicizia
to frighten spaventare
fritter la frittella
frog la rana
in front of davanti a/di fronte a
frozen food i surgelati
fruit la frutta
  fruit juice il succo di frutta
  fruit salad la macedonia
frying pan la padella
full pieno/a, completo/a
to function funzionare
funfair la giostra/la fiera
funnel l'imbuto
furnishings l'arredamento
furniture (piece of) il mobile

G
gallery la galleria
garage (for parking) il garage
  (for repairs) l'autorimessa
garden il giardino
garlic l'aglio
gas il gas
  gas cooker la cucina a gas
gate il cancello
to gather raccogliere
gentleman il signore
geography la geografia
German tedesco/a
Germany la Germania
to get angry arrabbiarsi
to get up alzarsi
gift il regalo
girl la ragazza

to give dare
to give (away) regalare
glass (for drinking) il bicchiere
  (material) il vetro
glasses gli occhiali
glove il guanto
glue la colla
to go andare
  to go away andarsene
  to go for a walk fare una
  passeggiata
  to go out uscire
  to go to bed andare a
  letto/coricarsi
  to go up salire
goat la capra
God Dio
gondola la gondola
good bravo/a, buono/a
goose l'oca
gossip le chiacchiere
to gossip chiacchierare
gram il grammo
grammar la grammatica
grandfather il nonno
grandmother la nonna
grape harvest la vendemmia
grapefruit il pompelmo
grapes l'uva
grass l'erba
Great Britain la Gran Bretagna
greatest più grande, massimo/a
Greece la Grecia
green verde
greengrocer il fruttivendolo
greens la verdura

grey grigio/a
grill la griglia/la graticola
grocer's la drogheria
ground il terreno
group il gruppo
to grow (something) coltivare
guest l'ospite
guide la guida
guitar la chitarra
gymnastics la ginnastica

H
hail la grandine
hair i capelli
  hair drier il fon/
  l'asciugacapelli
half la metà
ham il prosciutto
hammer il martello
hand la mano
handbag la borsetta
handkerchief il fazzoletto
handle la maniglia
to happen succedere/
  accadere
happiness la felicità
happy contento/a, felice
hard duro/a
hard disc il disco rigido/
  il disco fisso
hardware (computer)
  l'hardware
hardware (shop) l'utensileria
hardware (tools) la ferramenta
hat il cappello
to have avere

to have dinner pranzare/cenare
to have to dovere
head la testa
headache il mal di testa
headlight il fanale/il faro
healthy sano/a
to hear sentire
heart il cuore
heavy pesante
heel il calcagno
heel (shoe) il tacco
hello! ciao!
helmet il casco
help l'aiuto
to help aiutare
her suo/a
here qua/qui
to hide nascondere
high alto/a
hill il colle/la collina
his suo/a
to hit colpire
hobby l'hobby/il passatempo
to hold tenere
hole il buco/il foro
holiday la festa
holidays le ferie/la vacanze
holy santo/a
honey il miele
hook il gancio
horn (animal) il corno
(car) il clacson
hors d'oeuvres l'antipasto
horse il cavallo
hospital l'ospedale

hot caldo/a
hotel l'albergo/l'hotel
hotelier l'albergatore
hour l'ora
house la casa
how come
how much quanto
however però
hunger la fame
hurry la fretta
to hurt fare male
husband il marito
hut la capanna

I
I io
ice il ghiaccio
ice cream il gelato
ice lolly il ghiacciolo
idea l'idea
identity card la carta d'identità
if se
ill malato/a
illness la malattia
imagination la fantasia
to imagine immaginare
immediately subito/immediatamente
important importante
inch il pollice
including incluso/a
to increase aumentare
indeed infatti
independent indipendente
industry l'industria
inflation l'inflazione

information l'informazione
inhabitant l'abitante
inn la taverna/locanda
inquiry l'inchiesta
insect l'insetto
insecticide l'insetticida
inside dentro
instead invece
instrument lo strumento
insurance l'assicurazione
intelligence l'intelligenza
inter-city train il direttissimo
Internet l'Internet
Internet café l'Internet café
interesting interessante
international internazionale
invitation l'invito
Ireland l'Irlanda
iron (metal) il ferro
  (for clothes) il ferro da stiro
island l'isola
Italian italiano/a
Italians gli Italiani
Italy l'Italia

J
jacket la giacca
jam la marmellata
January gennaio
jar il barattolo
job l'impiego
joke la barzelletta/lo scherzo
jug il bricco
July luglio
to jump saltare
jumper il maglione

June giugno
just appena

K
keeper il custode/il guardiano
kettle il bollitore
key la chiave
kick il calcio/la pedata
to kill ammazzare/uccidere
kilogram il chilo(grammo)
kind (nice) gentile/cortese
  (type) la specie/il genere
kiosk il chiosco
kiss il bacio
to kiss baciare
kitchen la cucina
knee il ginocchio
knickers le mutande
knife il coltello
to know conoscere/sapere

L
lace il pizzo
laces i lacci/le stringhe
ladder la scala
lady la signora
lake il lago
lamb l'agnello
landing (stairs) il pianerottolo
landslide la frana
language la lingua
lantern la lanterna
large grande, grosso/a
last scorso/a, ultimo/a
  at last finalmente
late tardi

to laugh ridere
law la legge
lawn il prato
lawyer l'avvocato
leaf la foglia
leaflet il dépliant/l'opuscolo
lean (meat) magro/a
to learn imparare
least minimo
   at least almeno
to leave lasciare
left sinistra
leg la gamba
lemon il limone
to lend prestare
less meno
letter la lettera
lettuce la lattuga
level crossing il passaggio a
   livello
library la biblioteca
life la vita
lifeguard il bagnino
lift l'ascensore
to lift sollevare
light (weight) leggero/a
   (lamp) la luce
to light accendere
light bulb la lampadina
lighter l'accendino
lighthouse il faro
lightning il fulmine/il lampo
to like piacere
line la linea
lips le labbra
list la lista/l'elenco

to listen ascoltare
litre il litro
little poco/a
   a little un po'
live vivo/a
to live vivere/abitare
liver il fegato
livestock il bestiame
living room il salotto/
   il soggiorno
loan il prestito
lobster l'aragosta
locomotive la locomotiva
London Londra
long lungo/a
to look guardare
   to look after curare/badare a
   to look for cercare
lorry il camione
   lorry driver il camionista
to lose perdere
lost property office l'ufficio
   oggetti smarriti
love l'amore
to love amare
low basso/a
lozenge la pastiglia
luck la fortuna
lucky fortunato/a
luggage il bagaglio
   luggage rack il portabagagli
lunch la colazione/il pranzo
luxury il lusso

M
machine la macchina

mad pazzo/a, matto/a

magazine la rivista

to make fare/costruire/creare

male maschile

man l'uomo

management la direzione/
la gestione

manner il modo/la maniera

many molti/e, tanti/e

map la carta geografica/
la pianta

marble il marmo

March marzo

market il mercato

marriage il matrimonio

marrow la zucca

to marry sposarsi

marvellous meraviglioso/a

master (art) il maestro

matches i fiammiferi/i cerini

material (cloth) la stoffa/
il tessuto

mathematics la matematica

mature maturo/a

May maggio

mayor il sindaco

meal il pasto

meat la carne

mechanic il meccanico

medicine la medicina

to meet incontrare

meeting l'incontro/
l'assemblea/la riunione

melon il melone

member il socio/la socia

to mend aggiustare

menu (restaurant) il menù
(computer) il menu

message il messaggio

metal il metallo

method il metodo

metre il metro

microwave oven il forno a
microonde

midday il mezzogiorno

midnight la mezzanotte

military militare

milk il latte

milkman il lattaio

mill il mulino

minute il minuto

mirror lo specchio

miss la signorina

mist la nebbia

mixed misto/a

mixer il frullatore

mobile phone il telefono
cellulare, il telefonino

modem il modem

modern moderno/a

modest modesto/a

moment il momento

Monday lunedì

money il denaro/i soldi

month il mese

monument il monumento

moon la luna

moped il ciclomotore/
il motorino

morning la mattina/il mattino

mosquito la zanzara

mother la madre

mother-in-law la suocera
motor il motore
motor boat il motoscafo
motorbike la moto(cicletta)
mountain la montagna/il monte
mountaineer l'alpinista
mouse (animal) il topo
  (computer) il mouse
moustache i baffi
mouth la bocca
to move muovere/muoversi
movement il movimento
much molto/a
mud il fango
mule il mulo
mum la mamma
museum il museo
mushroom il fungo
music la musica
musician il musicista
my mio/a

N
nail (metal) il chiodo
  (finger) l'unghia
name il nome
napkin il tovagliolo/la salvietta
narrow stretto/a
nation la nazione
national nazionale
natural naturale
nature la natura
naughty cattivo/a, birichino/a
near vicino/a
necessary necessario/a
neck il collo

need il bisogno/l'esigenza
needle l'ago
nest il nido
net la rete
never mai
new nuovo/a
news la notizia/novità
newspaper il giornale/
  il quotidiano
  newspaper vendor il
  giornalaio
next prossimo/a
  next to accanto a/vicino a
nice bello/a, simpatico/a
night la notte
nightdress la camicia da notte
nine nove
no one, nobody nessuno/a
noise il rumore
noon mezzogiorno
north il nord/settentrione
nose il naso
not even nemmeno/neppure/
  neanche
nothing niente/nulla
novelty la novità
November novembre
now adesso/ora
nude nudo/a
number il numero
nurse l'infermiera
nut la noce/nocciola

O
objective la meta/l'obiettivo
to observe osservare

to occupy occupare
October ottobre
octopus il polpo
to offer offrire
office l'ufficio
oil l'olio
old vecchio/a
older people gli anziani
olive l'oliva
   olive oil l'olio d'oliva
omelette l'omelette
on su
   on purpose apposta
onion la cipolla
only (sole) unico/a, solo/a
open aperto/a
to open aprire
opera l'opera
opposite contrario/a,
   opposto/a
or o/oppure
orange (fruit) l'arancia
   (colour) arancione
orangeade l'aranciata
orchestra l'orchestra
to order ordinare
ordinary ordinario/a, comune
organ l'organo
origin l'origine
other altro/a
our nostro/a
outboard motor il
   fuoribordo
outside fuori
oven il forno
ox il bue

oyster l'ostrica

P
to package imballare
packet il pacchetto
to paint dipingere
painter il pittore/la pittrice
pair il paio
palace il palazzo
pale pallido/a
palmtop computer il palmare
pamphlet l'opuscolo
paper la carta
paraffin la paraffina
parapet il parapetto
parcel il pacco
parents i genitori
park il parco
parking place il parcheggio
party la festa
passer-by il/la passante
passport il passaporto
pastry la pasta dolce
patient il/la paziente
pattern il modello
pavement il marciapiede
to pay pagare
pea il pisello
peace la pace
peaceful tranquillo/a
peach la pesca
peanut l'arachide/la nocciolina
pear la pera
pedestrian il pedone
   pedestrian crossing le
   strisce pedonali

pen la penna
pencil la matita
pension la pensione
people la gente/le persone
  (nation) il popolo
pepper (seasoning) il pepe
  (capsicum) il peperone
percolator la caffettiera
perfect perfetto/a
perfume il profumo
perhaps forse
person la persona
to perspire sudare
petrol la benzina
  petrol pump attendant il
  benzinaio
pheasant il fagiano
philosophy la filosofia
photograph la fotografia
to photograph fotografare
physical fisico/a
piano il pianoforte
picture il quadro/l'immagine
pier il molo
pig il maiale
pill la pillola/la pastiglia
pillow il cuscino/il guanciale
pilot il pilota
pin lo spillo
pineapple l'ananas
pink rosa
place il posto/luogo
plan (of town) la pianta/
  la piantina
plant la pianta
plate il piatto

platform il binario/
  la piattaforma
to play (instrument) suonare
  (game) giocare
plum la susina/la prugna
plumber l'idraulico
pocket la tasca
point il punto/la punta
pole il palo
police la polizia
policeman il poliziotto/il vigile
politics la politica
poorly male
popular popolare
port il porto
post la posta
to post imbucare
post office l'ufficio postale
postcard la cartolina
poster il manifesto
posterior il sedere
postman il postino
potato la patata
pound sterling la sterlina
powder (cosmetic) la cipria
pram la carrozzina
prawn il gambero
precious prezioso/a
precise preciso/a
to prefer preferire
to prepare preparare/prepararsi
present il regalo/il dono
press la stampa
pretty grazioso/a
price il prezzo
to print stampare

prison la prigione
private privato/a
product il prodotto
profession la professione
program(me) il programma
pronunciation la pronuncia
proud orgoglioso/a
province la provincia
public pubblico/a, il pubblico
  public gardens il giardino
  pubblico
to pull tirare
pullover il maglione/il pullover
pumpkin la zucca
puncture il foro/la foratura
pupil l'alunno/lo scolaro
purse il portamonete
to push spingere
to put mettere
pyjamas il pigiama

Q
quality la qualità
quarter (of town) il quartiere
quarter of an hour il quarto
  d'ora
question la domanda
quick rapido/a, veloce
quickly rapidamente/
  velocemente
quilt il piumone

R
rabbit il coniglio
race la corsa
  (species) la razza

racket la racchetta
radiator il termosifone/
  il calorifero
radiator (car) il radiatore
radio la radio
rail la rotaia
railway la ferrovia
rain la pioggia
to rain piovere
rainbow l'arcobaleno
raincoat l'impermeabile
to raise alzare/sollevare
raisin l'uva passa
raspberry il lampone
rather anzi/piuttosto
raw crudo/a
to reach raggiungere
to read leggere
ready pronto/a
really veramente
rear il retro
recently recentemente/da poco
reception la ricezione
recipe la ricetta
record player il giradischi
recreation la ricreazione
red rosso/a
refrigerator il frigorifero
region la regione
religion la religione
to remain rimanere/restare
remains i resti
to remember ricordare/
  ricordarsi
to rent affittare
reply la risposta

to reply rispondere
republic la repubblica
residence la residenza
to rest riposarsi
restaurant il ristorante/
  la trattoria
  restaurant car la carrozza
  ristorante
restoration il restauro
to return ritornare/tornare
rib la costola
ribbon il nastro
rice il riso
right destra
  (fair) giusto/a, esatto/a
ring l'anello
to ring suonare
ripe maturo/a
river il fiume
road la strada/la via
roast/roast meat l'arrosto, la
  carne arrosto
rock la roccia
Roman romano/a
Rome Roma
roof il tetto
room la camera/la stanza
round rotondo/a, tondo/a
rubber la gomma
rucksack lo zaino
to ruin rovinare
to run correre
Russian russo/a

S
sack il sacco
sad triste
saddle la sella
sail la vela
sailor il marinaio
saint il santo
salad l'insalata
  salad bowl l'insalatiera
salary lo stipendio
salmon il salmone
salt il sale
  salt cellar la saliera
same stesso/a
sandals i sandali
sandwich il tramezzino/
  il sandwich
satisfied soddisfatto/a
Saturday sabato
sauce la salsa
saucepan la pentola/il tegame
sausage la salsiccia
saw la sega
to say dire
scales la bilancia
scarf la sciarpa
scene la scena
school la scuola
science la scienza
scissors le forbici
scooter la motoretta/
  il motorino
screwdriver il cacciavite
sculpture la scultura
sea il mare
season la stagione

seat il sedile
second secondo/a
secret segreto/a, il segreto
secretary il segretario/
  la segretaria
to see vedere
seed il seme
to seem sembrare
to sell vendere
seller il venditore
September settembre
serious serio/a
service il servizio
to sew cucire
sewer (drain) la fogna
sewing machine la macchina da
  cucire
shade l'ombra
shadow l'ombra
shape la forma
sheep la pecora
sheet (on bed) il lenzuolo
  (of paper) il foglio
shell (sea) la conchiglia
  (egg) il guscio
to shine brillare
ship la nave
shirt la camicia
shoe la scarpa
shop il negozio
  shop window la vetrina
shopkeeper il negoziante
shopping la spesa
short corto/a, breve
shoulders le spalle
to shout gridare

show lo spettacolo
to show mostrare/illustrare
shower la doccia
shrimp il gamberetto
side il fianco/il lato
to sign firmare
silence il silenzio
silk la seta
silver l'argento
simple semplice
to sing cantare
singer il/la cantante
single singolo/a
sink il lavandino/lavello/lavabo
sister la sorella
to sit down sedersi/
  accomodarsi
size (dimensions) la misura
  (clothes) la taglia
skates i pattini
to ski sciare
skier lo sciatore
skirt la gonna
skis gli sci
to sleep dormire
slender snello/a
slice la fetta
slide la diapositiva
slippers le pantofole
slow lento/a
small piccolo/a
smile il sorriso
to smile sorridere
smoke il fumo
to smoke fumare
snack lo spuntino/la merenda

snake il serpente/la biscia
to snore russare
snow la neve
so much tanto/a
soap il sapone
soccer il calcio
socks le calze
soft morbido/a
  soft drink l'analcolico/
  la bibita
software il software
soldier il soldato
sole (fish) la sogliola
sole (shoe) la suola
some alcuni/qualche/un po' di
somebody qualcuno
someone qualcuno
something qualcosa
somewhat piuttosto
song la canzone
soon presto/fra poco
sorry! scusi!/scusa!/scusate!
sound il suono
soup (thick) la minestra/
  la zuppa
  (clear) il brodo
south il sud/il meridione
souvenir il ricordo/il souvenir
space lo spazio
to speak parlare
special speciale
speciality la specialità
to spend spendere
spider il ragno
spinach gli spinaci
spirits i liquori

to split spaccare
sponge la spugna
spoon il cucchiaio
sport lo sport
sports field il campo sportivo
spring (season) la primavera
  (metal) la molla
square la piazza
squid il calamaro/la seppia
stadium lo stadio
stairs le scale
stamp il francobollo
to stand stare in piedi
star la stella
to start cominciare/iniziare
station la stazione
statue la statua
steak la bistecca
steam il vapore
steamer il vaporetto
steep ripido/a
steering wheel il volante
step il gradino/lo scalino
stew lo stufato/lo spezzatino
stick il bastone
still ancora
stomach lo stomaco
stone il sasso/la pietra
stool lo sgabello
stop (bus) la fermata
  to stop fermare/fermarsi
  to stop (doing something)
  smettere
storey il piano
story la storia
stove il fornello

straight diritto/a

strange strano/a

straw (drinking) la cannuccia

strawberry la fragola

stream il ruscello

street lamp il lampione

stress lo stress

stretcher la barella

string lo spago

student lo studente/
la studentessa

to study studiare

stuffed ripieno/a, imbottito/a,
farcito/a

stupid scemo/a, stupido/a,
tonto/a

style lo stile

suburbs la periferia

suddenly improvvisamente

sugar lo zucchero

suit l'abito

suitcase la valigia

summer l'estate

sun il sole

Sunday domenica

sunshade il parasole

superior superiore

supermarket il supermercato

surname il cognome

sweat il sudore

sweet la caramella/il dolce

sweetcorn il granturco/mais

sweets i dolciumi

to swim nuotare

swimming il nuoto

swing l'altalena

switch l'interruttore

Switzerland la Svizzera

symbol il simbolo

syringe la siringa

T

table il tavolo

tablecloth la tovaglia

tablet la compressa/la pastiglia

tail la coda

to take prendere/portare

tall alto/a

tap il rubinetto

tart la crostata

tax l'imposta/la tassa

taxi il taxi
taxi driver il tassista

tea il tè

to teach insegnare

teacher l'insegnante/
il maestro/la maestra

team la squadra/il team

teapot la teiera

teaspoon il cucchiaino

teleconference la teleconferenza

telephone il telefono

to telephone telefonare

telephone kiosk la cabina
telefonica

television la televisione
television set il televisore

temperature (heat) la
temperatura
(fever) la febbre

temple il tempio/la tempia

tent la tenda

terrace la terrazza
terrible terribile
thanks grazie
that quello/a
theatre il teatro
then allora/poi
there là/lì
thermal baths le terme
thermometer il termometro
thick spesso/a, denso/a
thief il ladro
thigh la coscia
thin magro/a
thing la cosa
to think pensare
thirst la sete
this questo/a
  this evening stasera
  this morning stamattina
  this time questa volta/
  stavolta
thousand mille
thumb il pollice
Thursday giovedì
ticket il biglietto
  ticket collector il controllore
  ticket office la biglietteria
tide la marea
tie la cravatta
tight stretto/a
tights i collant
till (shop) la cassa
time il tempo/la volta
timetable l'orario
tin (container) il barattolo/
  la scatola

tin opener l'apriscatole
tip la mancia
to tire stancare/stancarsi
tired stanco/a
tiring faticoso/a
toast (to someone) il brindisi
toaster il tostapane
tobacco il tabacco
tobacconist's la tabaccheria
today oggi
toe il dito del piede
together insieme
toilet il gabinetto/la toilette
tomato il pomodoro
tomb la tomba
tomorrow domani
tongue la lingua
too anche
  too much troppo/a
tooth il dente
  toothache il mal di denti
  toothbrush lo spazzolino da
  denti
  toothpaste il dentifricio
top la cima
torch la torcia elettrica
total (il) totale
tourism il turismo
tourist il/la turista
towards verso
towel l'asciugamano
tower la torre
town (large) la città
  (small) la cittadina
town hall il municipio/comune
toy il giocattolo

tracksuit la canadese/la tuta
tractor il trattore
trade il mestiere/l'esercizio
trader il commerciante
tradition la tradizione
traffic il traffico
   traffic lights il semaforo
trailer il rimorchio
train il treno
tram il tram
to transfer trasferire
travel il viaggio
to travel viaggiare
travel agency l'agenzia di
   viaggi
tray il vassoio
treasure il tesoro
trial il processo
triangle il triangolo
trifle (sweet) la zuppa inglese
trip il viaggio/la gita
trolley il carrello
   trolley bus il filobus
trousers i calzoni/i pantaloni
trout la trota
true vero/a
to try provare
Tuesday martedì
tuna il tonno
tunnel il tunnel/la galleria
turkey il tacchino
turn (shift) il turno
two due
type la specie/il tipo
tyre il copertone/la gomma/
   il pneumatico

U
ugly brutto/a
ultimately infine
umbrella l'ombrello
unbelievable incredibile
uncle lo zio
under sotto
underpants le mutande
to understand capire/
   comprendere
undress spogliarsi
unexpected imprevisto/a
unfortunately purtroppo/
   sfortunatamente
United States gli Stati Uniti
up su
to use usare
usual solito/a
utensil l'utensile

V
vacuum cleaner l'aspirapolvere
valley la valle
value il valore
van il camioncino/la furgone
vase il vaso
vegetables la verdura
vegetable soup il minestrone
vermouth il vermut
very molto/a, tanto/a
vest la canottiera
view il panorama
villa la villa
village il paese/il villaggio
vine la vite
vinegar l'aceto

vineyard il vigneto
violence la violenza
violet (la) viola
violin il violino
to visit visitare
vitamin la vitamina
voice la voce
  voicemail il voicemail,
  la posta vocale
volcano il vulcano
voltage la tensione/il voltaggio

W

wait l'attesa
to wait attendere/aspettare
waiter il cameriere
to wake up svegliarsi
Wales il Galles
walk la passeggiata
to walk camminare
wall (city) il muro
  (internal) il muro/la parete
wallpaper la carta da parati/
  la tappezzeria
to want volere
war la guerra
wardrobe l'armadio
to wash lavare/lavarsi
washing il bucato
  washing machine la lavatrice
wasp la vespa
watch l'orologio da polso
water l'acqua
waterfall la cascata
watermelon l'anguria/
  il cocomero

wave l'onda
we noi
weather il tempo
Wednesday mercoledì
week la settimana
weekend il fine settimana/
  il weekend
weight il peso
well (fine) bene
  (water) il pozzo
wet bagnato/a
wheel la ruota
  wheelchair la carrozzina/
  la sedia a rotelle
when quando
where dove
which quale
to whisper sussurrare
white bianco/a
who chi
whole intero/a, tutto/a
widow, widower la vedova,
  il vedovo
wife la moglie
to win vincere
wind il vento
window la finestra/il finestrino
windscreen il parabrezza
wine il vino
wing l'ala
winter l'inverno
with con
without doubt senza dubbio/
  senz'altro
woman la donna
wood (forest) il bosco

(material) il legno, la legna
wool la lana
word la parola
work il lavoro
to work lavorare
worker il lavoratore/l'operaio
world il mondo
to wrap up incartare
wreath la corona
wrist il polso
to write scrivere

y
year anno
yellow giallo/a
yesterday ieri
yoghurt lo yoghurt
you (singular) tu/lei
   (plural) voi/loro
young giovane
your (singular) tuo/suo
   (tua/sua)
   (plural) vostro/loro
   (vostra/loro)

z
zero zero
zip la chiusura lampo/
   la cerniera
zone la zona
zoo lo zoo

When you get back from your trip, try these **teach yourself** titles, available from all good bookshops and on-line retailers:

- **Teach Yourself One-Day Italian**
  Only 50 words and phrases to learn with a 75-minute audio CD and an 8-page booklet. Join Andy and Lis on their flight to Italy and listen in to the 'One-Day Italian Challenge'!

- **Teach Yourself Italian Starter Kit**
  Your personal tutor on two 70-minute CDs guides you through a 7-week programme. The coursebook, traveller's companion and flashcards make it easy.

- **Teach Yourself Instant Italian**
  Learn Italian in 6 weeks, on a daily diet of 35 minutes. There's a book with audio support on CD or cassette.

Thinking of buying a property in Italy? You'll need

- **Teach Yourself Buying a Home in Italy**, by Peter MacBride and Giulia Gigliotti
  The book will help you choose and buy a property abroad, and then will give you the words you'll need to help you restore or maintain it. 90 clearly labelled diagrams and help with the pronunciation on the essential language CD.